# Falling for Coastal Magic

## Stories of Southeast Georgia
by
Patricia Barefoot

*Patricia Barefoot*

Second Printing

# Falling for Coastal Magic

## Stories of Southeast Georgia

by

Patricia Barefoot

A Publication of

The Saltmarsh Press, Inc. of St. Simons Island

St. Simons Island, Georgia 31522

www.saltmarshpress.com

Designed by Coastyle Graphics & Publishing, Inc.
Cover Photograph by Barry Knapp
Printed in the U.S.A. by Morris Publishing
• 3212 East Highway 30 • Kearney, NE 68847

ISBN: 0-9666365-0-3

# Preface: To My Readers, A Very Personal Note

After grave consideration and much timidity, I submitted an essay in August, 1993 to the Brunswick, Georgia weekly *The Harbor Sound* for editor and publisher Jim Dryden to consider for publication. My intent was to somehow tell the story of a maligned soul whose life work was consumed telling a neglected story about the coastal landscape. Miss Mary Ross was, in the early 20th century, a student of our colonial Hispanic heritage and she devoted her life's blood to this pursuit. Today, her name has been memorialized by the city of Brunswick at the premiere Brunswick Harbor Market at Mary Ross Waterfront Park.

In order to learn more about the painstaking work of Miss Ross, I sought out her nephew, Captain Leo Ross of Brunswick. With his wife, Lois Ross, they have given freely of their knowledge and time. They have shared their precious memories of "Miss Mamie" and on many occasions, their recollections about life on the waterfront.

Following my conversation with the Ross family, I began to write stories about scholars, philanthropists, preservationists and other folks, whose past experiences largely contributed to the world that we should perceive and enjoy, today, in southeast Georgia. Some of these were "untold stories;" there are, yet, many more to tell in documenting the richness of our coastal past.

Encouraged by my former major professor Dr. Charles M. Hudson of the Anthropology Department at the University of Georgia, I determined that people, places, events, and oral history interviews would be fruitful ground for telling and sharing stories with the coastal community. Oldtimers shared their vast wealth of knowledge. Always my intent has been to nurture and cultivate our peculiarly southern 'sense of place.'

Raised in a family who relished story-telling, and surrounded by so many interesting characters, I have eagerly pursued a life-long, abiding interest in the historic past. In particular, my late paternal grandmother, Mrs. Henry J. (Ruby Ray) Cofer encouraged and abetted my natural inclinations.

I spent innumerable hours with Grandmother in her old tabby hotel which was once located at the St. Simons Pier. Along the way, I met and interacted with a diversity of visitors and guests who stayed at the "Golden Isles Hotel." Among others, Tallu Fish and the late coastal historian, Margaret Davis Cate colored my perceptions. Only much later did I learn that the autocratic Cate shared many relatives with my maternal family. She has been a guiding light and ever present in my quest.

When I was a child, it was not the "Village" to us, but the "Pier," and today the circumstances and conditions are quite different when my Cofer, Parker, Sasser and Goebel cousins enjoyed frolic on the sand beaches near our Grandmother's business. Our friends were members of the Hice, True, Knight and McCaskill families, some of whose descendants live today and thrive on the Island that we treasure in immemorable ways.

Our families instilled in us a reverence for the very unique spot that we call "HOME" and, no doubt, each one of us, today, holds this close to our hearts. We've all gone our separate ways, but a commonality of interest endures.

Often, I ponder the prose of Sidney Lanier's poem which immortalized the spreading marshes of Glynn. "Free by a world of marsh bordered by a world of sea." Vastly rich in natural resources, we all should each day express gratitude for our abundance, both in people and in natural resources.

If in some small way, this collection of essays contributes toward our appreciation and understanding, it will have achieved my objectives, and I am indeed grateful for anyone whose eyes pass this way.

## About the Author

Patricia Barefoot is a life-long resident of Glynn County, Georgia. After completing an M.A. in Anthropology at the University of Georgia, she joined the U.S. National Park Service at Fort Frederica where she continues to serve. Her feature articles on coastal history and culture, from which this selection has been made, were first published in *The Harbor Sound*, James Dryden, publisher.

# Acknowledgements

In my efforts to identify the legacies described here, I have come to meet and work with many talented and dedicated librarians, archivists and historians and book lovers who share my enthusiasm.

Dr. John Christian, Miss Winnie Wainwright and Mrs. Katie Cooler of the Bryan-Lang Historical Library in Woodbine.

Mrs. Frances Davenport Kane, Director of the St. Simons Public Library; the late Mrs. Dorothy Houseal, Miss Marcia Hodges and Mrs. Diane Jackson of the Brunswick-Glynn County Regional Library.

Frank Wheeler, Assistant Director of the Georgia Historical Society.

Mrs. Linda Orr King, Mrs. Pat Morris and Bob Wyllie of the Coastal Georgia Historical Society and Museum of Coastal History.

Donald O. Davis, president of the Huxford Genealogical Society in Homerville, and Ed Mathews, a coastal photographer.

Bill Rivers and Mrs. Jackie Edwards of the Hofwyl-Broadfield Plantation State Historic Site.

Richard and Gini Steele, photograph historians from Beaufort, South Carolina. Virginia Hobson Hicks, proprietor of Brunswick's Book Shop.

Tribute and thanks also to the many friends who talked with me about their families. Among others: Mrs. George C. Cook, Jr. and Fred Cook; the late Margaret Tait Ratcliffe, Mrs. Howard (Lawrenna) Powell and Charles Tait, Jr.; Mrs. Mattie Gladstone; Miss Clara Marie Gould, Mrs. Howard Scott and Mrs. King (Beverly Wood) Hart; the late Mrs. Viola Hummings and Mrs. Phorestine Appling; Jasper and "Miss Candace" Barnes;

To my friends and colleagues: Miss Mary McGarvey and Miss Joyce Blackburn. To Tom Wallace, a special expression of gratitude for his constancy and good will in assisting with vital computer activities.

To Mr. James Dryden, publisher of *The Harbour Sound*, and his General Manager, Sally D. Rinear, who were the first to publish these essays and so many more!

A deep appreciation and love to my parents, Mr. and Mrs. Sam Cofer who cultivated a 'sense of place' and my maternal uncle, the late Melvin G. "Bud" Joyner, a great storyteller.

I dedicate this volume to my husband and helpmate, Forrest "Frosty" Barefoot.

# Table of Contents

## Early Preservationists

## An Agrarian South

# Living in the Past

# Coming of Age

# Early
# Preservationists

# Georgia's Historian:
# Lucian Lamar Knight

*Hazzard Vault near burial spot of Lucian Lamar Knight*
*Christ Church Graveyard*

Born in 1868 in Atlanta, to Clara Daniel and Captain George
Walton Knight, Lucian Lamar Knight benefited from an education in
the area public schools and, in 1888, graduated from the University of
Georgia as his class valedictorian. With the death of his father,
Knight's uncle John Benning Daniel provided the paternal interest and
financial assistance.

For over a decade after graduation, Knight worked for his cousin
Henry Grady, editor of the *Atlanta Constitution*, as a reporter; his
work was characterized by its historical nature: humor, poetry, editori-

*3*

als and eulogies. His free time was spent in a study of Georgia's past, a life-long venture that culminated in his appointment as the state's first official historian.

Along with his career in journalism, Knight studied law. But in 1902 he left these for the time being and entered Princeton University where he earned a degree in theology. In 1905, Lucian Lamar Knight, now ordained a minister, accepted an associate pastorship in Washington, D.C. at the Central Presbyterian Church. The clergy was not to be his calling after all and within two years he had returned to Atlanta where he became managing editor of the *Library of Southern Literature*, a series published by Martin and Hoyt Company. Simultaneously Knight released his edition of *Reminiscences of Famous Georgians* in 1907.

Now Knight's career as a proponent of Georgia's history accelerated. In 1913, he brought out the two volume *Georgia's Landmarks, Memorials and Legends*. There he set down a tribute to his muse, "the patriotic women of Georgia, the guardians of Georgia's immortality whose work reminds the present that little in the way of life's true riches can be promised to us by a future, however golden, at the expense of an unremembered past."

That same year, Knight accepted an appointment as Georgia's official archivist; within five years he had begun the publication of the classic *Colonial Records*. In that decade alone, he wrote and edited *Georgia's Landmarks* and the six volume *A Standard History of Georgia and Georgians*. In due course, Knight became the first state historian, then Director of the Georgia Department of Archives and History. At his retirement in 1925, he was designated state historian emeritus. Lucian Lamar Knight died in 1933 and is buried at Christ Church, Frederica, St. Simons Island. If you would know the man, read the epitaph on his tomb:

*Scholar, historian, orator, poet, First state historian of Georgia Founder of the State's Department of History and author of many Important works relating to the history of the Commonwealth.*

*For more than forty years a ruling elder in the Presbyterian Church Among the old families of the Island.*

*Sleeping where the first guns were planted by the Great Founder for*
*The protection of the Colony and where the issue Between Spain and*
*England, for the Conquest of a Continent, was at last settled among*
*Whom I wish to sleep in the long peace of eternity under the boughs*
*Of the Wesley Oak, and by the waters of the murmuring Altamaha,*
*Asking no sweeter epitaph than this;*
*Here lies one who loved Georgia, every page of her history and every*
*Foot of her soil.*

# The Redoubtable Margaret Davis Cate: A Coastal Historian

*Photo courtesy Margaret Cate Collection
Georgia Historical Society, Savannah*

Certain character traits come to mind when I think about the late, great coastal historian and preservationist, Margaret Davis Cate. She possessed the ultimate 'sense of place' and cultivated a deep, abiding appreciation of our richly diverse coastal heritage. Generously and eagerly, she shared her deep knowledge of coastal history with guests at the famed Cloister Hotel when she lectured there.

Uncanny foresight served her well. Mrs. Cate and photographer Orrin Sage Wightman documented true African-American funerary art at the Bowens family cemetery in Liberty County, Georgia. Today, this graveyard art is mostly just a memory. Only the out-of-print classic, *Early Days of Coastal Georgia* by Cate and Wightman portrays the richness of the visions of Cyrus Bowens and the complexity of his art work.

Fiercely loyal to family, Mrs. Cate could be a formidable ally to others as well, or sometimes a foe. Her straightforward autocratic style often masked the grim determination with which she prosecuted historic inquiry and preservation concerns. Possibly her crowning achievement was the dominant role that she played in the establishment of Oglethorpe's town at Frederica as a national monument.

Born in Brunswick, Georgia on 24 November, 1888 to John Bentson and Ida Stafford Davis, little 'Maggie' was educated in county schools. In 1905, she received the distinction of being the first honor graduate to matriculate at historic Glynn Academy. Her formal education at the University of Tennessee summer school prepared her for a teaching career that spanned the years 1905-1917.

In 1917 she married widower Dr. Gustavus Vassa Cate, a prominent Brunswick physician. Until 1932 the Cates owned and operated a lucrative poultry farm at Touchstone Ridge where they raised the noted Cate strain of Barred Plymouth Rock hens. Margaret continued the poultry operation after Dr. Cate's death. In 1937 her prized hens were certified as the first flock in Georgia free of the dread pullorum disease. Buyers included four state agricultural colleges and the fledgling USDA in Beltsville, Maryland.

Mrs. Cate discontinued her poultry operation in 1943 when she accepted the position of postmistress on Sea Island, Georgia. We glimpse the practical, pragmatic side of her in correspondence addressed to Judge Folks Huxford in Homerville, Georgia in June, 1944. "By this you will see that I have moved from Brunswick. It was a hard pull for me to leave. I have lived there for 54 years and never wanted to live elsewhere...However, my work is at Sea Island and it is nothing but sensible for me to move over here...am cutting every tie that bound me here. All of this is because of two things—it is a sound move economically and I believe it will give me the time necessary to write my book."

The Cate papers reflect that her genealogical inquiries were legion. Largely with the help of Judge Huxford, the wiregrass genealogist, Mrs. Cate investigated and documented both paternal and maternal lines of descent. On May 18, 1931 when she applied for membership in the Brunswick chapter of the National Society of the Daughters of the American Revolution, Margaret claimed matrilineal descent through Sibbiah Earl Blair, a supporter of the patriot cause. In her letter of June 23, 1939 to Judge Huxford, she wrote, "William Blair and Sibbiah Earl Blair served in the Revolution as well. I went into the DAR on Sibbiah's record, and was very proud to be able to prove service for a woman ancestor."

In 1934 Cate, the genealogist, assumed the role of chapter historian with the Brunswick DAR, a position which empowered her to interpret and promote our coastal heritage. She encouraged the erection of markers and monuments proclaiming the richness of our coastal history. Later, as county historian, she wrote the text for most of the Georgia state commission markers that dot our landscape and are of more than casual interest to visitors on the Golden Isles. Her key role on the Glynn County historic landmarks commission prepared Cate, the historian, to serve as general chairman of the historical pageant that she orchestrated in July, 1936. Held at Shadman Field, present day Oglethorpe Park, this signal event celebrated the bicentennial anniversary of the founding of Fort Frederica. Oldtimers relish the memory of this notable event and recall the zeal with which Mrs. Cate pursued the preservation of the beloved fort at Frederica. The handsome official program of the event stated: "Live with us, ye dauntless spirits of the past, and make us worthy of the heritage upon which we have come, that our state, founded on Wisdom, Justice and Moderation, may endure forever!"

A lifetime of community service and activism ended abruptly with Mrs. Cate's death on November 29, 1961. A shocked coastal community mourned her loss and offered their eulogies. Let us not forget the pioneering spirit of Margaret Cate! Long may her legend, her memory, and her sweet inspiration live!

# The Legacy of Mary Ross

*Photo courtesy the Ross Family*

Oglethorpe Bay? For those history buffs familiar with the Brunswick waterfront, it holds an intriguing legacy. Just glance at engineer G.R. "Lummie" Baldwin's 1837 map of the port city! Find that, in fact, Oglethorpe Bay includes those salty seawaters which lap along the shores from Downtown, and running seaward to just east of the 1950s-style Sidney Lanier Bridge.

Let's explore the legacy of historian and preservationist Mary "Miss Mamie" Ross. Locals will quickly recognize the Ross name as belonging to the shrimp-fishing family who harvest their bounty aboard the

"Miss Bernice II", one of the oldest trawlers docked along the waterfront. Owned by Capt. Leo Ross and his oldest son, Andy, their trawler continues a family legacy closely connected with the sea.

Capt. Leo's paternal aunt, "Miss Mamie" Ross should be a familiar figure, not only to newcomers, but to all coastal Georgians who have delved into the contributions of early 20th century area notables. Ross rubbed elbows with the likes of historians Margaret Davis Cate, Bessie Lewis, and Tallu Fish, Board of Trade promoter Ruby Berrie, and philanthropist, Cator Woolford.

Mary Letitia Ross was born in Camden County in 1885 to Caroline Mehrtens and John Dilworth Ross. Reared in the port city, Ross graduated from Glynn Academy in 1898. The continuation of her education at the State-Normal school, Athens, prepared her to teach in the Glynn County school system until 1910 when she moved southwest to Tucson. Later, she resumed her studies at the University of Chicago, majoring in geography. At the University of California, Ross was awarded two degrees, one an M.A. in History, based on a graduate thesis titled "The Anglo-Spanish Conflict in the Caribbean Area and the North American Mainland, 16th-17th Centuries."

Her mentor, Herbert Eugene Bolton, collaborated with Ross for over twenty years, and quite likely Ross's research contributed to his work in various if unrecorded ways. Today, recognized as the "father" or pioneer of the "Spanish Borderlands" school of historic interpretation, Bolton's career is a well-respected one.

His innovative method of comparative analysis focused on the importance of the Church and the military garrison in shaping the designs of a sprawling Spanish Empire. In 1922, Bolton predicted that his protege "Mary Ross will put Spanish Colonial Georgia on the map....and be the historian of the Anglo-Spanish contest for Georgia."

In 1925, Bolton and Ross jointly published a controversial book titled *The Debatable Land* which examined Spain's claim to the land of flowers-- "La Florida" which included present-day Georgia. Unfortunately, in this (a "must" read for students of early Georgia!) and in subsequent scholarly articles authored by Ross, certain tabby ruins were identified as evidence of Spanish architecture dating to the 1600s. Thus, grew the myth associated with limey tabby ruins, and mysterious Spanish missions. In 1937, a rising star in Georgia history, E. Merton Coulter of the University of Georgia edited a book titled

*Georgia's Disputed Ruins.* Published under the auspices of the greatly esteemed Georgia Society of the Colonial Dames of America, it refuted the "tabby mission theory" and a myth about tabby ruins located in McIntosh, Glynn and Camden Counties.

Its publication heralded the death knoll of Ross's future publishing prospects as "the historian of Spanish Georgia." Regrettably, her former mentor Herbert Eugene Bolton proved no saviour. In addition, Mary Ross bore the brunt of criticism because of her "romantic theory about the origin of certain tabby ruins."

In fact, after the book's publication inflammatory news articles followed in the Atlanta papers, and largely due to this criticism, Ross never again published in academic circles. But she never lost her yearning to learn more about the influence of Spain in the southeastern United States and how that presence enriched our lives.

Reared to appreciate the value of an education, Ross pursued a life-long quest to assemble an enviable collection of documents about her beloved Spanish Colonial Georgia.At the urging of Carroll Hart of the Georgia Archives, after Mary Ross's death, the Ross family donated her papers to the State.

It is a treasure trove of archival research materials, encompassing some 750 items, which Ross painstakingly retrieved from the Archives of the Indies, Seville, Spain. In addition, it includes over 300 other documents from institutions, family and other personal papers.

In a precocious way, Mary Ross shaped our world as we envision it today, filled with lovely Spanish Mediterranean Revival architecture, ideally suited to the humid, subtropical coastal Georgia climate. On the islands, its presence dominates the landscape and is a reminder of coastal comfort, sans electrical convenience.

In her retirement, she lived at 1518 Norwich Street and meticulously maintained the eastern portion of Hillary Square, with the help of the Morgan children, General Lee, John Henry and Dianne.

The City Park and Tree Commission recognized Ross's devotion to the beautification of Hillary Square by dedicating "that park on the east side of Norwich Street, between the Chevrolet used car lot and the residence of the late Mary Ross." The late secretary Mrs. A.C. (Ruth) Quarterman stated "We have received many favorable comments from various people in the city, concerning attention to this park over the years. It is through the assistance to the city by the people of Brunswick that the parks can be kept presentable."

In April, 1982 the Park and Tree Commission desired to re-dedicate a "Mary Ross Park" within city boundaries, due to the expansion of business into the 1500 block of Norwich St. On September 7, 1988 the City Commission renamed the "Mary Ross Waterfront Park" in her honor, formally dedicated in July, 1989.

# Camden's "Miss Bebe" Lang: Historian & County Archivist

*Photo courtesy of Mrs. Henry E. Williams & family*

What a wonderful legacy "Miss Bebe" Lang bequeathed to her native Camden County and to all coastal Georgians after her retirement from Georgia's Department of Archives. Those who visit the Bryan-Lang Historical Library located in the courthouse complex at Woodbine, will discover a wealth of material about our history and heritage.

According to her namesake and niece, Mrs. Henry (Bebe) Williams Sr. "Aunt Bebe and her best friend and colleague, Mary Givens Bryan, always wanted to write a book about Georgia. Later, Aunt Bebe made up her mind that she wanted an archival library in Woodbine." It took four years of local, grass roots fundraising spear-

*15*

headed by Camden historian Eloise Bailey Thompson before Camden folks raised sufficient monies to build that library. Dedicated on November 8, 1987, the Bryan-Lang Historical Library includes books, county records and several important special collections including the papers of the Coastal Highway District and those of H.J. Friedman Sr, the highway engineer. The personal papers of Ruby Berrie of the Board of Trade are stored in the library as are the early records of the Fort Frederica Association.

Born at Satilla Bluff on March 23, 1903 to Rufus Sumner Lang and Beatrice (Dufour) Lang and descended from Isaac Lang Sr., Beatrice Fairchild "Bebe" Lang claimed membership in one of Camden's oldest families. Bebe's father, Rufus Lang, was a businessman who operated a general store and brokered timber. He served his county as a commissioner and as a state senator. A close-knit Lang family must have nurtured her sense of business practices and political savvy; her mother, Beatrice, instilled a deep sense of the importance of history in making life's choices.

At the river village of Satilla Bluff, the livelihood of most settlers was dependent upon the Hilton-Dodge Lumber Company, its saw mill, cross-tie cutting, turpentine extraction and the production of naval stores from the piney woods. These were the days of rafting logs from the interior to the mills, of turpentine stills, of steam-powered waterborne vessels such as the "Atlantic" and the "Hildegarde." A regular route up the big Satilla past Woodbine and on to Owen's Ferry and Burnt Fort provided for the needs of folks who resided in a very remote rural setting.

Yet, in the decade before Bebe's birth, Satilla Bluff had already begun its decline because of the decreased mill work and, in 1893, the arrival of a railroad three miles farther up the river. This transportation artery irretrievably sealed the fate of the river village and signaled the creation of the municipality of Woodbine out of the one-time J.K. Bedell rice plantation.

From her niece Bebe Williams, we learn that "All the Lang children enjoyed a happy childhood--the general store was the focal point. Aunt Bebe was an outdoors person. She loved to ride horses; she hunted woodland creatures. But she also could arrange boxing matches for the entertainment of her neighbors."

Bebe attended college at Valdosta State for four years. In 1925, she married and moved to Eastman in Dodge County, but she returned to Woodbine when the marriage went sour.

*16*

When the Coastal Highway, later called Highway 17, opened, Bebe perceived a business opportunity and so opened a gas station on the corner of Fourth and Bedell Avenues in Woodbine. When the Second World War began, she moved to Jacksonville, Florida to work on an assembly line at Cecil Field in support of the war effort. She lived in this "bold new city" until 1947 and then moved back to Woodbine to look after her invalid mother who eventually died three years later.

Now Bebe turned to a career as Camden County's Registrar and simultaneously as a Justice of the Peace in Military District 31. In 1952, Georgia Secretary of State Ben Fortson dispatched the newly appointed Director of Georgia Archives, the indefatigable Mary Givens Bryan, to Woodbine, her mission: to collect, preserve and microfilm historical and county records under the auspices of a county archives section. The focus at first was on the original eight counties: Wilkes, Richmond, Burke, Effingham, Chatham, Liberty, Glynn and Camden and the preservation of their documentary histories. Mary Givens Bryan was known to "live, eat and breathe history." Her infectious enthusiasm is summed up in her claim: "There is more romance in history than one can imagine." The serendipitous meeting of these two lively ladies, Lang and Bryan had grand results for them both.

In 1956, Bebe Lang became the director of the state's county archives section which meant a move to Atlanta/Decatur to assume awesome responsibilities as she travelled across the state collecting and preserving the official records of Georgia's one-hundred and fifty nine counties. For the next twenty years, she maintained a major source of Georgia's rich heritage of local history.

After retirement and until her death in 1989, Bebe Lang made her home in Decatur. Having let it be known that she wanted a permanent site for the library and special collections she had compiled, she influenced friends in Camden who raised the funds for the Bryan-Lang Historical Library.

Miss Bebe's sister, Mrs. Don (Dorothy Lang) McCaskill of St. Simons Island, together with our friend, the wonderful Bebe Lang, belonged to an informal society of women of great courage and foresight: Mary Givens Bryan, Margaret Davis Cate, Tallu Fish, Ruby Berrie, Bessie Lewis and Mamie Ross. Their 'sense of place' has made our lives richer, surrounded as we are by the results of their effort to preserve the historic monuments, the materials, the records of the families of Georgia.

# Educator & Master Story Teller: Martha Mizell Puckett

*Photo courtesy of Mrs. Howard Powell, Sr.*

Until her death on July 8, 1974, civic activist, gifted story-teller and educator Martha Mizell Puckett worked for the benefit and education of youth in Brantley, Wayne and Pierce Counties. For those of us who benefited from the role models of the Misses Jane Macon, Lula Howard, Beulah Lott or Bernice Tracy, the cut of fabric is quite similar. In short, they dedicated their lives to the betterment and education of the youth of southeast Georgia.

Born on March 26, 1897 near Lulaton to Jasper P. Mizell and Susan Matilda Purdom Mizell, Martha was raised in the Great Satilla River basin. In her popular book titled *Snow White Sands*, published posthumously (1975), the story about "our family garden" reveals her reverence for nature's bounty and the central role that the garden played in family and community affairs.

"The Family Garden contributed beautifully to my life in all areas of work, pride, profit, health, joy, vision, duty, necessity, charity, thrift, fertility and care of the soil, seed sowing and improvement...Our garden was a continuous process."

These reminiscences provide insight into Martha Puckett's life-long dedication to the goals and objectives of the 4-H Club. The importance of such a modest institution is apparent in the genius of Wayne County's first county agent, J.P. Shedd and Home demonstration agent Annie Bennett. Their work foreshadowed the formation of the national 4-H Club when, in 1912, they established a local Corn club and Canning club. The purpose was to improve the living standards of a rural population by teaching prevailing wisdom about cultivating the soil, animal husbandry, and better food preservation.

In 1956, Shedd presented Martha Puckett with a national 4-H Club Alumnae award in recognition of her achievements and as a charter member of the fledgling canning club. He recalled Mrs. Puckett's "down to earth practical wisdom" as an asset to his county agent work. Displaying a distinct pride in her southern heritage, Mrs. Puckett told about the importance of corn as the staff of life for southern folk and how they lived off cornbread. From these circumstances, she derived her creed or motto: "We learned first of all to make the best that we had better."

Martha Puckett's father served in prominent leadership positions in his county, in addition to being a circuit-riding hardshell Primitive Baptist preacher. His route extended from the Wayfair Church, located on Hard Shell Church Road near Plum Orchard Cemetery, McIntosh County to Pigeon Creek in Nassau County, Florida. Her childhood experiences at the Smyrna Primitive Baptist Church near Lulaton (Brantley Co.) where many members of the Mizell family rest in the graveyard, greatly influenced Mrs.Puckett.

Educated in a single-room log cabin school, Martha Mizell absorbed her studies, and heeded the emphasis that her parents placed upon education. Of the Strickland School: "There were never stale moments. If your mind reached out, your teacher was right there beside you to help you reach as far as you were capable of going."

In December, 1912 she completed her early schooling, and in 1913 at the age of fifteen years took and passed a teacher's examination. Subsequently, she accepted a teaching position at the remote Burnt Bay School. Transportation to her first assignment was by horse and buggy, train, and ox cart. "I rode an ox cart with high wooden wheels into the Okefenokee Swamp to Burnt Bay School." Under these humble circumstances, Martha Mizell began a 50-year classroom career. In December, 1920 she married railroad contractor Lawrence P. Puckett. In addition to raising their family and balancing the demands of a career with home, Mrs. Puckett continued her education at the University of Georgia. During summer breaks, she completed six years of post-secondary training. Both as teacher and principal Mrs. Puckett served in many one-room schoolhouses, prior to her assignment to a school located in the Empire community where she taught for 11 years.

In time, she worked for six years in the Gardi community, four years in Odum, five years in Patterson, the last five years of her education career were at the old Jesup Junior High School. Dedicated in February, 1994 the Martha Puckett Middle School, located off Durrence Road in Jesup, stands today as tribute to Puckett's substantial contributions to the enlightenment of youth.

In *Snow White Sands*, Mrs. Puckett evoked memories in simple terms: recollections about old-fashioned gallberry brush brooms for cleaning the front yard, candy pullings, community sings, ingatherings and tin wash basins for a foot washing sacrament, cane grindings, butterbean and pea shelling, gardens of plenty, hickory smoked sugar cured hams, hog killings and seasoned hickory cured sausage, and long handled gourds for drinking water. Her folksy wisdom and long tales reveal a woman whose rich life experiences enlivened her imagination and zeal for teaching truths to her wards, and inculcating pride in the heritage of Georgia's pioneer settlers. In spite of great change in the southeast Georgia landscape and lifeways, Mrs. Puckett maintained a staunch enthusiasm for the lessons of yesteryear. Her sage advice speaks of her essence when she wrote, "Make the best that you have, better."

# Mrs. Ruby Wilson Berrie:
# A Charming Ambassadress of the Golden Isles

*From the "Ruby Berrie Collection"*
*Bryan-Lang Historical Library, Woodbine*

Let us not forget an important promoter of Good Will for Brunswick-Glynn and a close personal friend and confidant of the late, great coastal historian Margaret Davis Cate. Known as a charming ambassadress of Georgia's Golden Isles, Mrs. Ruby Berrie's distinguished career included forty-seven years of dedicated community service.

Born on December 1, 1893 in Atlanta to Jennie Lind Stewart and James Grant Wilson, Ruby Berrie resided in Glynn County for 75 years. A torn and tattered Class of 1912 program revealed a tantalizing piece of her personal history. Among Ruby Angeline Wilson's fellow graduating classmates were Mallery King Aiken, May DuBignon Stiles and Clara Miriam Krauss.

In time, Miss Wilson married Kenneth G. Berrie, a Brunswick native and a veteran of World War I. His stable and upwardly mobile position as an employee of the Brunswick Post Office assured her of a certain degree of comfort.

When she was 21 years old Ruby began her life's work to promote commerce at the old Brunswick Board of Trade. In 1921, she served as its secretary with her office in the Oglethorpe Hotel. Renamed the Chamber of Commerce in 1946, the old Brunswick Board of Trade witnessed successive elected presidents, with Mrs. Berrie as secretary and office manager.

I have on hand an essay about Brunswick, written by this lady in which her sense of history shines. "As far back as 1737, when the duty exacted from vessels clearing Brunswick Harbor was a pound of pistol powder a ton, Brunswick Harbor was considered by the English as one of the best and safest harbors on the continent." She continued with a description of the port City's geographical location, population, and availability of railroads, steamship lines, highways, air lines and industries.

Impressive statistics were at her command. For instance, she noted that Brunswick was "a little lumber town on the coast" in 1875. But, she asserted, "in the last decades of the 19th century, the port became a natural outlet for the rich products of Georgia's famous pine belt; by 1900, the value of its commerce had rocketed to $24 million."

She recalled the early importance of shipbuilding at the port, especially the war effort of building Liberty ships during World War II. "The annual volume of business generated by the two shipbuilding plants in 1944 amounted to $107, 330,000."

A keen view of her contributions to our community may be gleaned from the proceedings of a testimonial dinner held at The Cloister Hotel in November, 1961 which honored Ruby Berrie's retirement on November 15, 1961 after serving 47 years with the Brunswick-Glynn County Chamber of Commerce, 1914-1961. Elected secretary-emeritus and assured that "the chamber's doors will always be open to her," past chamber presidents honored her with numerous accolades. Local businessman Wylly O'Quinn, Jr. chamber president 1952-1954 recalled "Mrs. Berrie has taught through example that perfection is the only standard."

Presided over by the late A.W. Jones, Sr., a highlight of the banquet was the presentation to Mrs. Berrie of a sterling silver tray, as a token of appreciation from chamber members. The inscription recognized "her magnificent service and untiring efforts toward the growth, development, and enhancement of Coastal Georgia in her work with the Chamber of Commerce."

One observer of her career noted her presence as featured speaker at an awards banquet for 600 Garden Club enthusiasts held on Jekyll Island in 1962. "She has done everything from sending recipes for Brunswick Stew to answering inquiries about Glynn County to begging Washington for milk during World War II shortages".

Ruby Berrie was an active member of the Brunswick DAR, and served for many years as secretary of the Fort Frederica Association. Linkage to Frederica deepened both her friendship and camaraderie with Margaret Cate. On November 16, 1969 a resolution of the Association recognized her great efficiency as secretary, and commended her for untiring efforts in her work with the historic collection at the Cate library.

When Ruby Berrie died in March, 1983 her estate included a collection of historic memorabilia, donated to the Bryan-Lang Historical Library by Judge Alex Williams. According to library director, Dr. John Christian, "Mrs. Berrie's valuable collection of coastal historic materials is an important asset to the library." It consists of six file drawers of historic information primarily on Glynn County, and the activities of the Board of Trade, and the minutes of the Fort Frederica Association. Seek her there.

# Judge Folks Huxford:
## Historian & Genealogist of the Pioneers of Wiregrass Georgia

*Photo courtesy the Huxford Genealogical Society*

On November 16, 1893, a rare individual was born in Coffee County, Georgia, to Calvitt and Kansas Drawdy Huxford. In his lifetime, Folks Huxford achieved status as a jurist, historian, Baptist minister, lawyer, musician, journalist, genealogist and public servant: a man for all seasons.

Many Georgians know the Judge for his promotion of the genealogy and history of the pioneers of "Wiregrass Georgia," which really means all of South Georgia. In his August 1950 column in the *Alma Times*, Judge Huxford defined "wiregrass Georgia" as the original counties of Wayne and Irwin.

This territory in its original formation extended from the Altamaha and Ocmulgee Rivers on the North to the Florida line and from the two coastal counties of Glynn and Camden westward to the old county line of Early County as defined in 1818.

Map enthusiasts will discover this territory reached from the seashore to the current Alabama line in southwest Georgia, about one-half of Georgia's coastal plain.

Waycross author Caroline Miller won the 1934 Pulitizer Prize for her novel *Lamb in His Bosom* which popularized the lives and ways of the "wiregrass." This tale of piney woods settlers contrasted their hardships and privation with the sumptuous style of the coastal cotton aristocrats.

In 1952, Judge Huxford characterized these gritty pioneers. "They braved dangers untold, endured hardships and suffered privations without end, lived under the most primitive conditions, made a way where there was no way; learned by the hard way the great lessons in life of hard work, thrift, frugality, self-reliance, resourcefulness, courage, independence and faith in God."

Not long before his death on March 21, 1981, Judge Huxford helped found the Huxford Genealogical Society. Notable colleagues in this venture included the late Mrs. Charles C. (Geneva Edenfield) Stebbins, Jr. of Darien; Mr and Mrs. Morrell A. Knight and Mrs. Beth Engel of Brunswick; Mr. Jack E. Ladson, Jr. of Vidalia and Miss Leila Summerall of Waycross.

Judge Huxford agreed that since early childhood his consuming interest in history guided his perceptions and conversations. On the other hand he admitted that his inability to grasp the fundamentals of algebra accounted for his leaving school in the eighth grade!

Gifted with a photographic memory, however, at age sixteen the young man sought work in the Clinch County Courthouse where he "read the law" and where he happened to memorize all of the land-titles given to the first settlers in the County. In 1920, the Georgia Bar Association admitted him to that august body.

At the county courthouse in Homerville, the impressionable young lawyer seized every opportunity to talk with Confederate Army veterans. Their great stories not only sharpened his passion for history but resolved him to describe the family histories of those rural folk whose past would otherwise go untold. In 1916, just twenty-three years old, Huxford published his *History of Clinch County* and though it was not a financial success, this did not detract him from his real vocation.

Judge Huxford travelled among courthouses in North and South Carolina and Georgia searching for documents such as wills, deeds and landgrants, those institutional records which accounted for the lives of the "wiregrass ancestors." He recorded oral traditions, visited churches and cemeteries, gathered genealogical materials from newspapers and family Bibles. In 1951 he published the first edition of *Pioneers of Wiregrass Georgia* which was based upon some 335 family sketches assembled over a lifetime of devoted research. Across the next generation, seven additional volumes of the *Pioneers* were printed, featuring over three thousand sketches of south Georgia individuals. Along the way he inspired *The Georgia Genealogical Magazine* and wrote a *History of Brooks County* and established a weekly column in the *Valdosta Daily Times.*

The Huxford Genealogical Society continues this scholar's work through the growing Huxford Genealogical Library and a quarterly magazine. The tenth volume of the *Pioneers* series is soon to appear. E.L. "Boe" Williams, Jr. of Valdosta, a member of the Board of the Huxford Society, claims that "Judge Huxford was the smartest man I ever knew! The Judge was giving, compassionate and an unselfish researcher who never asked anything in return. He put 'meat on the bones' when he recreated those early wiregrass pioneers. I remember when he played Amazing Grace on the piano, he made grown men cry!"

# "Always Tallu:" Tallu Fish — Jekyll Island's Preservationist

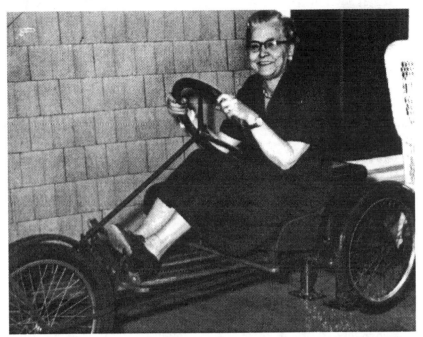

*Photo courtesy Mrs. Howard I. (Tallu Fish) Scott*

There is a marker in the Jekyll Island Museum that tells us of Tallu Fish who "kept the history of the Island in the public eye." Lest we forget. It is this writer's privilege to recall some of Mrs. Fish's efforts to promote and preserve the memorabilia of a bygone era on Jekyll. In the 1950's, for instance, when my grandmother, Mrs. Henry Cofer, hosted the St. Simons Woman's Club in her tabby Golden Isles Hotel, Mrs. Fish often came by with copies of her book, *Once Upon an Island: The Story of Fabulous Jekyll.*

Grandmother Ruby confirmed that Mrs. Fish was a very important person and her book a vital introduction to Jekyll's history for all Georgians: "The weathered oaks of Jekyll spread their arms around a pageant of memories, holding them safe in timeless enchantment...For now it is an island of the people, by the people and for the people."

What a lovely thought - a timeless, enchanted island! Surely when little Tallu spent summer vacations on St. Simons in the cottages of the old Waycross colony, she must have dreamed about her special island. From her daughter, Tallu Scott: "My mother remembered vividly taking the "Emmeline" or the "Hessie" to St. Simons. She always tried to catch a glimpse of the secret and romantic life on Jekyll that she imagined!"

Born on August 31, 1901, in Waycross, Ware County, to Minnie Margaret (Brinson) Jones and Wylie Newton (W.N.) Jones, Tallu Jones attended local schools and later Georgia State College for Women in Milledgeville. In 1920, she married Edward Arthur Fish whose travels as a road engineer with the Highway Department required his family to be flexible. While residing in Gainesville, Tallu Fish continued with her education, receiving in 1933 a degree in journalism from Brenau College. Her career as a writer began with *The History of Lamar County* composed while she and Ed Fish lived with their children in Barnesville. An inspiration was Jack Williams, editor of the *Waycross Journal*.

During the Great Depression, Ed and Tallu Fish lived in Ed's hometown, Williamsburg, Kentucky. Tallu freelanced with the United Press International and the Associated Press while contributing a column to the *Louisville Courier-Journal* called "United We Stand" which chronicled the activities of The United Federation of Women's Clubs throughout Kentucky. Ed Fish died in 1953, and a year later, Tallu Fish settled on Jekyll Island, owned by the State of Georgia and soon connected to the mainland by the Jekyll Island Bridge, which enabled visitors to flock to the old "millionaire's playground." Tallu Scott: "My mother wanted to give the people of the state of Georgia a taste of what it was like to be a millionaire. She devoted her every working moment to learning about the history of Jekyll."

With the substantial organizational skills gleaned from club activities and given her fascination with local politics, she went to work collaborating with Bebe Lang, County Archivist. The veteran journalist wrote the 'script' for many of the historical markers erected on Jekyll. This contribution came to the attention of Atlanta columnist Celestine Sibley who commended Tallu's efforts to promote for modern Georgians an "enchanted island" as a legacy of the Edwardian Age.

Tallu Fish lived in the Rockefeller Mansion, "Indian Mound" for eight years. For a time after World War II, state prisoners were incarcerated in an iron-barred barn located off Jekyll's Riverview Drive. When Mrs. Fish moved into "Indian Mound" she found the prison 'arsenal' secured in the Rockefeller safe! While operating the museum installed in the Rockefeller home, while maintaining the furniture and other artifacts of an earlier age, she managed to produce a chatty cookbook called *A Pretty Kettle of Fish: Jekyll Island Seafood Cookery* which originally sold for one dollar and is now a collector's item. In 1963, she privately printed *Sidney Lanier: America's Sweet Singer of Songs and the Author of the Marshes of Glynn and Other Poems*, designed by Bill Haynes of the Ashantilly Press. She also assembled a priceless scrapbook for each of the years, 1954-1970, she lived on Jekyll.

In 1970, the archives collected by Tallu Fish were given by her family to the Museum. And there is "Tallu Fish Lane," an honor bestowed by the Jekyll Island Authority.

A sense of community was nurtured by those pioneers who settled in the newly acquired state park after World War Two. Mrs. Fish enjoyed the company of Dell Walker Massey of Colonel's Island and the Dewey Scarboros who restored and furnished the Walter Jennings home "Villa Ospo."

The vision Tallu Fish had of a restored historic district on Jekyll Island has been realized in the long-term goals of the Jekyll Island Museum. She was indeed in the vanguard of the modern preservation movement.

*Photo by the author*

# Philanthropist Cator R. Woolford of the Retail Credit Company

*Photo courtesy Mrs. Howard I. (Tallu Fish) Scott*

Community planners have envisioned a North Glynn County Regional Park as an attractive amenity near a "new" C.B. Greer Elementary School. Unquestionably, the concept merits attention as an element in the "greenspace and quality of life" issues. But there is a precedent worth noting and that is the generous tract of land donated for a public park along the Altamaha rice fields near Elizafield Plantation.

The Ruby Berrie Collection in the Bryan-Lang Historical Library in Woodbine shed considerable light on the energetic activities of a Georgian who left great footprints on the sands of Glynn County: Cator R.Woolford.

Woolford was born in Cambridge, Maryland, in 1869 where he was educated in local schools and then at a military academy attached to the University of Maryland. When he was eighteen, Woolford joined the Weather Bureau of the U.S.Army Signal Corps, serving thereafter in Chattanooga for three years. In time, he took a commission in the Tennessee State Militia and rose to the rank of Colonel of the Third Regiment.

Simultaneously, Woolford worked for the Tennessee Mutual Building and Loan Association until 1897 as an assistant secretary-treasurer. From there, he moved into the family business already launched by his brother: Woolford and Company, a retail grocer and participated with great relish in the Retail Grocers Association. He soon organized the Retail Credit Company which specialized in consumer credit reporting and also published a *Merchants Guide* subscribed to by major insurance companies. Incorporated in 1913, the RCC became a national institution within two years. Such was the remarkable success of the Company that Mr. Woolford's financial circumstances remained quite sound across the Great Depression.

In the mid-1930s, Woolford presented 350 acres of the Elizafield tract to the State of Georgia. Operated as the "Santo Domingo State Park" by the Georgia Forest Service, it was transferred in 1946 to BOYS ESTATE. The current stewards can make use of the trails, tabby ruins and buildings still standing.

Woolford was familiar with the immediate region having purchased Altama Plantation in 1933 whose 6500 acres became his home until his death in 1944. Once owned by the  planter extraordinaire, James Hamilton Couper and called "Hopeton-Altama," the plantation had fallen into disrepair after the Civil War and passed through the hands of several owners including a family of Ohio Shakers and one William "Willie" DuPont of Wilmington, Delaware.

In the last years of his life, Woolford promoted Georgia's coast and touted the quality of life in Glynn County. Known as "Mr. Caty," Woolford's enthusiasm for the history and romance of the region found expression in a fledgling Tri-County Historical Landmarks Commission formed in 1935. The mission: the identification and marking of sites of historical significance in McIntosh, Glynn and Camden Counties. Of particular interest were ruins of tabby structures. The first officers of the Commission were Woolford, Chairman; Margaret Davis Cate, vice-chairman and Ruby Berrie, secretary-treasurer.

A year later, the Glynn County Historic Landmarks Commission sponsored a bi-centennial pageant held at Shadman Field (now Oglethorpe Park) on St. Simons Island.

The Brunswick Board of Trade and the Commission successfully lobbied for congressional legislation which created the Fort Frederica National Monument in May 1936.

Prosperity enabled Cator Woolford to concentrate his vision on civic endeavors. In Atlanta, he introduced vocational guidance and dental health services in the public schools.

He cooperated with the Julius Rosenwald Foundation in its program of educational advancement for African-Americans. The Georgia College Placement Office and the personnel office of the University of Georgia were Woolford's pet projects. His friendship with FDR prompted his part in the financing of a Georgia Hall at the Warm Springs Foundation promoted by the President.

As a public-spirited philanthropist, "Mr. Caty's" good works contributed toward the preservation of antiquities.

# Mary Wylie McCarty:
# A Woman of Achievement

*Photo courtesy Mrs. Howard I. (Tallu Fish) Scott*

When she was a high school senior in Waycross, Mary Wylie
Jones interviewed the legendary "Queen of the Okefenokee Swamp,"
Lydia Stone of Cowhouse Island for a school paper. Mary's father,
Wylie Newton Jones, owned a retail shoe store in Ware County at that
time and it's likely that as his daughter sat down to talk with "The
Queen," she knew that her subject wore a size 12 shoe! This essay
foreshadows Mary Wylie's career as a journalist and publicist.

Mary Wylie Jones was born in Waycross on December 4, 1903, the
third of four girls born to Wylie and Margaret Jones: Kathleen, Tallu
and baby Cecille who later in life would characterize their south
Georgia childhood as a "wonderful, wonderful one." In an era when

southern women were not encouraged to pursue a higher education, Mary Wylie nonetheless prospered. She graduated from Georgia State College for Women in 1922 with an honors degree in education and turned to a teaching position in Waycross. (Her history of her alma mater, later named Georgia College, would appear in a 1972 fiftieth anniversary program.)

Not long after returning to Waycross, Mary Wylie was offered a job in public relations in Atlanta by Cator Woolford of the Retail Credit Company. One early project given her was the preparation of a directory of special programs offered by American colleges and universities; this required considerable travel about the eastern seaboard.

Her career as a publicist prospered across that decade. Not long after her marriage to Atlantan Edwin F. McCarty in 1931, her mentor, Woolford, recommended her to Mr. Howard Coffin of the Sea Island Company. Subsequently, Mary Wylie created and edited *The Cloister Bells*, a rotogravure magazine devoted to the unique heritage of coastal Georgia and to the many distinguished guests who visited Coffin's hotel, The Cloister.

During the five years with Sea Island Company, Mary Wylie shared a cottage with her sister, Cecille, and her husband, Carey Sutlive, who was City Editor of *The Brunswick News* and the author of a popular column called "Suts Sports Spots." In time Sutlive went to work in Washington, D.C. with the Lend Lease Program.

When she retired from her publicist position in 1935, Mary Wylie received a letter of "lamentation" from Howard Coffin who extolled her term of service with Sea Island. She would always be a member of the "family." Moreover, "Not only will you find the latchstring on the outside, but a lamp in the window as well."

In Atlanta, Mrs. Edwin F. McCarty made a tremendous contribution to civic and service organizations. Her editorship of *Garden Gateways* and presidency of the Atlanta Cherokee Garden Club are remembered. She reorganized and expanded the Junior League School of Speech Correction which became a model for similar institutions, and was cited as a worthy memorial to her career by historian Franklin Garrett. In 1956, she was recognized as "Woman of the Year in Education."

Mary Wylie McCarty died in 1992. Her niece, Tallu Fish Scott offers this epitaph: "My aunt was a shrewd businesswoman. She combined a sense of dignity with great Southern charm." *The Cloister*

*Bells* is long out of print but editions can be found in special collections libraries around the state, The University of Georgia, for instance. A collection of essays on Georgia history, *Flags of Five Nations*, includes some of her works.

# Mrs. Sutlive's
# "Gone With the Wind" Scrapbook

A while ago, Mrs. Cecille Jones Sutlive sat down with some friends who wanted to look at her treasured *Gone With The Wind* scrapbook and hear about the premiere of the film at Loew's Grand Theatre in Atlanta on December 15, 1939. That had been a signal event: large crowds, bright lights, politicians and movie stars! Margaret Mitchell thought: "We will never see the town so excited again!"

*The Atlanta Constitution* claimed that the premiere had "attracted the largest group of dignitaries to Atlanta since President Roosevelt made his 1932 campaign speech in the civic auditorium." These dignitaries shared the limelight with Atlanta's elite and movie celebrities at the Gone With The Wind Ball! Governors Rivers of Georgia--Cone of Florida--Maybank of South Carolina--Dixon of Alabama and Cooper of Tennessee. Movie stars Clark Gable with his wife, Carole Lombard; Vivien Leigh; Ona Munson ("Belle Watling"); Laura Hope Crews ("Miss Pittypat"); Ann Rutherford and Evelyn Keyes (Scarlett's sisters), Olivia de Havilland and Leslie Howard!!!!

The night before, the Atlanta Junior League sponsored a ball with music by the popular Kay Kyser Orchestra. A keepsake was the "Junior League Gone With The Wind Premiere Ball Program" replete with photographs of the stars and advertisements from local businesses. The program proclaimed (in patriotic terms) the book as "The Greatest Literary Phenomenon of Modern Times."

Mrs. Sutlive watched the film from the third row in company with her sister and brother-in-law, Mr. and Mrs. Edwin McCarty. From there they went off to a breakfast (1-3am!!) hosted by the Piedmont Driving Club!! And then home to the scrapbook.

There we find articles clipped from the Atlanta press which argued that the Junior League Ball was "By Far The Most Brilliant In The History of Atlanta" where the elite of Atlanta and the screen world mingled "amid rich pageantry."

Another feature proclaimed "Guess Who. It's Scarlett O'Hara at the Ball. If you don't already recognize her, she's lovely Vivien Leigh, the Scarlett of Margaret Mitchell's famous novel." The author, by the way, later expressed her pleasure at the part being given to the "charming" British actress but she disdained the selection of Clark Gable as Rhett Butler!!

On the matter of an Englishwoman taking on the part of an American woman, President-General Mrs. Walter D.Lamar of the United Daughters of the Confederacy "completely endorsed Miss Leigh."

No question about it! It was a three day, star-studded never-to-be-forgotten event which placed Atlanta "in cinematic history as the site of the biggest, most star-studded world premiere of the most publicized, most eagerly awaited and subsequently most beloved, most seen movie picture of all time."

Fifty years later, 4,000 Atlantans flocked into the Fox Theatre to commemorate the 50th anniversary of the premiere. The first time, patrons paid $10.00. In 1989, the ticket cost $100.00!!

And there it all is, in Mrs.Sutlive's precious scrapbook: GWTW In Atlanta!!

# An
# Agrarian South

# Olive Cultivation in Coastal Georgia

In the deep Old South, few farmers or planters cultivated cash crops on a large-scale. Among those agricultural commodities grown by the planter class were corn, long staple or "sea island" cotton, sugar cane, rice and indigo. In the memory of many people, only rice and cotton formed the basis for plantation agriculture.

Restricted in a geographical sense to coastal cultivation, both rice and long-staple cotton enabled a small, elite group of the planter class to realize enormous profits. Of course, there were bad years too, very bad years. But for the well-to-do progressive agriculturist, access to ready cash and cash flow created a mind-set amenable to experimentation.

Open vistas suggested lavish lawns, sub-tropical and tropical flowers, shrubs, vineyards, orchards and fruit trees. Under these circumstances, certain early agronomists ventured to plant experimental crops, such as the imported French olive. In a spirit of competition and by listening to the sage advice of Thomas Jefferson, some planters eagerly embraced olive cultivation.

In his *Farm Book*, this visionary statesman and philosopher wrote "The greatest service which can be rendered any country is, to add a useful plant to its culture; especially, a bread grain; next in value is oil." Jefferson desired the popular acceptance of olive culture for the production of oil and for the relief of mankind. He considered olive oil a "proper and comfortable nourishment" in the flavoring of vegetables.

In a letter of March 22, 1804 written to his Marseillaise friend, Stephen Cathalan, Jefferson referred to coastal Georgia planter "John Couper of St. Simon's island in Georgia [who] now proposes to undertake it, and being led to it by inclination, and a gentleman of property, in the most favorable situation, he will give the culture a fair trial. He has been informed of the superior excellence of the olive of Marseilles."

Located on the northend of St. Simons Island, John Couper's plantation was at "Cannon's Point," named after the colonial tradesman Daniel Cannon. Widely known as a progressive agronomist and thinker, Couper imported a variety of exotic plants into the sub-tropics of southeast Georgia. He wrote extensively in period publications to report on his results and successes.

In July 1828 Couper wrote to the editor of the popular journal *The Southern Agriculturist* to remark on the culture of the Olive Tree. He noted that olive cuttings must be "at least one inch in diameter" to effectively root. He customarily set out the trees twenty-five feet apart, and inter-cropped potatoes. In the bitter freeze of February, 1835 Couper lost hundreds of olive trees, but his upbeat report did not anticipate such devastation.

"I am told that on Cumberland Island there are many bearing Olives, and that there are also several trees of large growth near Beaufort, and even in Charleston." (Couper, no doubt, meant the terraced gardens at Dungeness, on Cumberland Island.)

In 1803, Caty Littlefield Greene Miller (Mrs. Phineas Miller) and her family moved into a newly completed four-storied tabby home. Surrounded by fields of long-staple cotton and sugar cane, the Millers eagerly acquired and cultivated a wide variety of exotic plants. Near the main house, "terraced gardens bordered by silvery olives trees" led the way to a boathouse and landing.

In 1849, historian George White published an intriguing book titled *Statistics of the State of Georgia*. In the section devoted to Glynn County, he included a letter by John Couper's son, James Hamilton Couper, originally read at a meeting of the South Carolina Agricultural Society.

By mid-century the younger Couper had gained great experience in olive culture. He felt that the lower Southeastern seaboard would prove "as suitable for the cultivation of the olive as the south of France."

He had calculated that 25 trees to an acre of land was a suitable ratio, and 50 trees to an acre if not inter-cropped. "The product of oil varies very much with the size of the tree, the character of the soil, and the fruitfulness of the season." A news article of February 7, 1880 reported on Island olive culture. "There are trees (olive trees) on this island that have borne continuously for the last fifty years."

Finally, certain legacies of the land still appear today in roadways, landmarks and spacious yards. For instance, a county roadsign beckons to passersby at "Olive Way," near the present U.S. Coast Guard Station at East Beach. Known today only to old-timers, on the northend of the Island bordering on Jones Creek at Cannon's Point is a bluff known as "Olive Grove."

On the southend of the Island, the Cater-Armstrong-Postell family once lived on a 1,600-acre plantation called "Kelvin Grove." Part of their legacy is a very old shrubby and silvery-leafed olive tree that grows in the spacious yard of Mrs. W. B. Willis, at Kelvin Grove. Olives, a source of sustenance and a symbol of peace.

# Floyd's Neck and an Anchor-Shaped Tabby House

Camden County records reveal the acquisition of large tracts of land through King's grant and purchase by Revolutionary War Colonel Charles Floyd and his only child, General John Floyd. By 1809 these transplanted Carolinians had enlarged their holdings to encompass 5,825 acres on which they cultivated cotton, indigo and rice fields, and elaborated a substantial maritime business.

Young John's five-year apprenticeship as a carpenter prepared him to craft keelboats and shallow draft two-masted schooners from the abundant live oak timber. Such design was especially useful for plying shallow, shoaling waterways through the southeast coastal trade routes. Frontier resourcefulness, plantation crops and their lucrative shipping enterprises account for the Floyds' accumulated wealth.

The Floyds' patriotism is clear. They reserved two hundred acres south of Bellevue for a military "parade ground" and to train Georgia militiamen in coastal defense. Among other distinctive military exploits, during the War of 1812 General John Floyd commanded a force of 600 men at Point Peter, Camden County.

Floyd served two terms in the state legislature, both as representative and state senator, and in 1826, he represented his district in Congress. Today, a north Georgia county proudly boasts the name "Floyd" in recognition of his contributions to early Georgia.

Eventually, a live oak and cedar lined mile-long road connected the two adjoining plantations Bellevue and Fairfield at Floyd's Creek where General Floyd built his home. (His father, Colonel Charles Floyd,died in 1820 and is buried with his wife Mary Fendin Floyd in the Fairfield family burial plot.)

In January 1823, "Yankee workmen" began the two-year long construction of an "anchor-shaped" tabby house at Bellevue . Eight-foot high tabby walls formed the foundation for a cypress upper story. Side-flanking piazzas supported by round columns faced spacious lawns, a vineyard and an orchard. A semi-circular drawing room framed the view of Mrs. John Floyd's (Isabella Maria Hazzard) one/half acre formal rose garden. She presided over the lavish care devoted to the abundant flowering trees, shrubs and bulbs, many of which were imported from the Caribbean.

Close-knit family members occupied their leisure time with outdoor recreation, including competitive shooting, horse racing, fishing, hunting and banquets. The Floyd's "Camden Hunting Club" frequently hosted other planter families and members of the "St. Simons Agricultural and Sporting Club." Among the amenities of an active social life were the famed racing regattas.

In June 1839 General John Floyd died. His will stipulated that his widow Isabella retain life estate in Bellevue. When she died twenty years later, Bellevue and its plantation lands reverted to Floyd's estate. Both Bellevue and Fairfield plantation houses were a casualty of the War Between the States.

Today, an imposing marble obelisk and lengthy epitaph mark the resting spot of General Charles R. Floyd, grandson of the first Charles Floyd, son of John, a military man of acknowledged ability, a poet, a musician, and a painter who died at age 48 years on 22 March, 1845.

Nearby cathedral oaks line the sandy road that leads to the Fairfield family burial ground where Gen. John Floyd and other family members rest. One mile distant in a field of broom sedge stand the thick tabby walls of an anchor-shaped house, fashioned after the Floyds' debt to the sea.

The last Floyd to live at Bellevue was Pompey Floyd, a former slave who may have arrived in 1859 on the Georgia coast aboard the infamous schooner, "The Wanderer" and who, "after freedom," purchased 100 acres of land from Samuel Floyd. Bordering Todd's Creek, a tributary of the Satilla, Bellevue remained intact from about 1802 until 1927 when Mrs. Rhoda Floyd, Pompey Floyd's widow, sold the property to Mr. Howard Coffin.

Located within the boundaries of the sprawling agricultural chemicals complex owned by Rhone-Poulenc, S.A., the anchor-shaped house is "one of the largest ruins of an early nineteenth century tabby structure in coastal Georgia."

# John Houstoun McIntosh
# and His Sugarworks

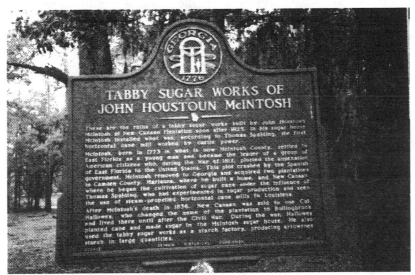

On January 19, 1736 a group of Scot Highlanders settled on Barnwell's/Lower Bluff at New Inverness (Darien). Led by John McIntosh Mohr, a descendant of the Borlum branch of the McIntosh family, these intrepid fighters proved the difference in the struggle for early Georgia. At first called "St. Andrew's Parish," a reflection of their Old World ancestry, on December 19, 1793 this coastal county was renamed "McIntosh" by the state legislature in honor of the contributions of this distinguished military family.

When the family patriarch's youngest son George McIntosh died in 1779, his considerable wealth passed to his seven-year-old son, John Houstoun McIntosh whose given name, middle and surname reflect the Scot penchant for tribute to ancestors. The young McIntosh rose to the occasion and carried on the family tradition of business savvy and leadership.

Today, three historic Camden County plantations bear the mark of McIntosh's ownership: Refuge, Marianna and New Canaan Plantations. By a King's grant to his father, George and then through inheritance, John Houstoun McIntosh acquired Refuge Plantation, where he brought his bride Elizabeth Bayard to live in 1792.

Located along the north banks of the Satilla River, near present-day Woodbine, Refuge Plantation was a 500-acre tidal rice plantation, which became at times of Indian raids, storms, and other threats, a place for refuge.

Later, McIntosh settled in Spanish East Florida and acquired large tracts of land where he continued his planter activities. On December 29, 1810, John Houstoun McIntosh of Fort George Island, East Florida purchased 850 acres on the St. Mary's River from Samuel and Letitia Humphreys of Southwark, Pennsylvania.

Embroiled in a sensitive political scenario, McIntosh abandoned his lands in East Florida, and reaffirmed his allegiance to the United States. In 1813, he moved to the St. Mary's area, and in 1819 purchased Marianna Plantation where he built a large rectangular wooden plantation home on brick pillars with impressive octagonal spire-like wings on each end.

About one mile distant were "good planting lands" at the northern end of Dark Entry Swamp. McIntosh called these hammock lands, New Canaan Plantation and planted sugar cane. His selection of a site for cane planting has been attributed to John Couper, of Cannon's Point, St. Simons Island who wrote, in 1829: "Our best Cane lands will be our inland swamps, where they can be kept dry in the fall of the year." Today, both Marianna and New Canaan Plantations are mostly absorbed by the sprawling Naval Submarine Base at King's Bay.

Still, observant passersby who travel the Crooked River Road will notice a state commission marker near the main gate to King's Bay. It simply states "Tabby Sugarworks of John Houstoun McIntosh." The sign is the consequence of environmental impact studies and funding for an archaeological excavation of the McIntosh sugarworks derived jointly from the Camden County and the King's Bay Impact Coordinating Committee. In 1985, the Georgia Department of Natural Resources, Office of Historic Preservation published a booklet, edited by John R. "Chip" Morgan on *Intensive Archaeological Testing at the John Houstoun McIntosh Sugarhouse, Camden County, Ga.*

Based on the excavation and interpretive work of Tom Eubanks of the University of Florida, Gainesville, this insightful report stemmed from his intensive archaeological testing in September/October, 1981 and his investigation of the social history of sugar production in the Americas. His research design examined "the extent, nature and significance of the ruins" of this 19th century sugarhouse.

The imposing nature of these tabby ruins dominates the wooded landscape. Standing tabby walls 14' high and with a thickness of 14" "define a rectangular building with three large rooms and two porches," and a total floor space of 6,450 square feet. Today, historians credit John Houstoun McIntosh with constructing the first animal-powered horizontal sugar mill in Georgia. Equally intriguing to the substance of the tabby ruins is how McIntosh came to build them, and the 1930s controversy over these "disputed ruins." Were they evidence of a former Spanish mission? Their age dates to 1825/1826 because prior to 1825, sugarhouses were generally octagonal or circular and accommodated vertical roller mills; therefore, they were not examples of the Spanish mission period.

At the encouragement of Thomas Spalding of Sapelo Island, many coastal Georgia planters diversified their agricultural crops by adding "ribbon cane." In his extensive writings on plantation agricultural products, Spalding recommended crop rotation with cotton and potatoes because of their deep roots and subsequent friable soil.

His first cousin John Houstoun McIntosh was the direct beneficiary of Spalding's conscientious investigations. Not only were the tabby sugarworks constructed by the "Spalding method," but Spalding claimed it was at his suggestion that McIntosh built "the first horizontal mill ever worked by cattle power."

Many authorities credit Thomas Spalding in the early 19th century with reviving tabby, as an enduring, stucco-like building material, a coastal concrete. A key ingredient in the Spalding method of tabby construction was the use of old, whole oyster shells. Then, the shells, leached of salt, were mixed with equal parts of lime, pit sand and water, and poured into plank form boards and allowed to harden.

# The Morrison Plantation
# In Camden County

History buffs quickly recognize the names of Retreat, Cannon's Point, Hampton and West Point Plantations, large long-staple cotton producing tracts possessing a worldwide fame. Some students of history will associate Altama, Evelyn, Grantley and Broadfield with the cultivation of a healthful and delicious grain, rice.

In the days prior to the American Civil War, many planters avidly nurtured cash crops, such as rice, cotton, corn, cane and indigo. Monies derived from sales on an international market afforded many of these planters a lavish life-style.

But other plantations flourished in McIntosh, Glynn and Camden Counties beyond those located along the tidewater reaches, and on St. Simons Island. For instance, the tidewater rice plantation called "Refuge" was located on the northern banks of the Great Satilla River. This large tract was inherited in 1780 by John Houstoun McIntosh, grandson of John McIntosh Mohr, chieftain of the Highlanders who settled Darien.

Not far from Refuge was the Morrison Plantation, owned by John Morrison and located on the south side of White Oak Creek, Camden County. Circumstances surrounding this cotton and corn plantation piqued my interest; a search for additional information about the old Morrison place shed considerable light on the interconnectedness of coastal history.

Purchased by banker, speculator, legislator and planter, Thomas Butler King in 1831, Waverly Plantation was located just north of the Morrison place. But by late winter, 1842 King's declining finances forced the sale of Waverly's cotton and rice-producing lands. In fact, a coastal paper of March 5, 1842 posted notices of "U.S. Marshal's sales of 246 slaves and nearly 20,000 acres in three counties to satisfy judgments against King."

Similarly, Camden County records such as census data, marriage records, deeds of record and wills document changes in household and transfer of properties by the Morrison family. The Fourth (1820) U.S. Census, Camden County simply recorded George Morrison, between 26-45 years of age engaged in agriculture.

On January 3, 1824 the last will and testament of George

Morrison, Sr., which disposed of his worldly estate, was recorded in *Camden County Will Book* A:320-321. Beneficiaries were his nephews George Morrison, Jr. and Ignatius, and his beloved brother John Morrison of South Carolina.

These relatives were heirs to a few African slaves and a stock of horses, cattle and hogs. In addition, he bequeathed two tracts of land, including 250 acres on the St. John's River, Spanish East Florida, and a tract of 150 acres on the St. Mary's River.

In May 1825 John Morrison and George, Jr. applied to court for an order authorizing sale of human chattel to John Houstoun McIntosh. Sold at the courthouse in Jefferson for $1450 and the payment of debts were Ned and his wife Tamer and their four children, Daniel, Stephen, John, and York who subsequently died and a fellow named Harry.

Other Camden County records noted the marriage of Susannah Wright and George Morrison Jr. on September 4, 1823 and Charlotte E. Lawrence and John Morrison on December 20, 1866. These early settlers consistently occur in the census records from 1830 and we can infer certain things about their livelihood and conditions. For instance, in the 1830 census district encompassing St. Mary's, White Oak and Red Cap, George Morrison, between the ages of 20-30 years, was listed as head of household. His unnamed wife's age was between 15-20 years, and three children, under five years of age included two girls and one boy.

By the Sixth U.S. Census, Morrison's growing family included eight children, his wife and an unnamed male between 40-50 years of age. Population figures for Camden in 1845 included 5,482 inhabitants, and of that number 1,721 white and 3,761 black. This reflects typical black majorities for coastal areas where both rice and cotton were cultivated by the planter elite.

In July, 1845, Morrison a shrewd businessman, purchased about 400 acres from Jonathan Gouldren of Lowndes Co., Georgia for $300. Situated on the north side of the Great Satilla River on the Tower Swamp, this parcel contained 195 acres of swamp/hammock, and 215 acres of well timbered pinelands. Originally granted to Major Simon Fraser of Liberty County, Morrison sold in August 1845 to Duncan L. Clinch for a tidy profit at $900.

Only by the 1850 census did the enumerators collect increasingly sophisticated information about residents. For instance, a 46-year old

George Morrison, planter born in South Carolina was head of household of ten individuals. They included his 42-year old wife Susan (Susannah), and their children Matilda (22); Mary Ann (18); John (16); James (14); Sarah Ann (12); Abner (11); Charity (9) and Abithae (7). At age 40, Susan/Susannah gave birth to their youngest child, Aribella.

In the 1860 census, planter George Morrison's household was dwindling in size, possibly due to marriages and/or deaths. His wife Susan was 52 years old and three siblings remained at home, John H. a planter 25 years old; James D., planter 23 years of age and sister Charity, 18 years of age.

Susan appeared as head of household in the 1870 census and her son James, age 36 years was living at home. On October 12, 1870 he married C.C. Crum whose family owned the Crum Plantation in the sandhill section of Camden, and today part of the McCarthy family's substantial holdings.

Also, in the 1870 census John, Charlotte, and their children Marion, two years and David, one year old appeared in a separate household enumerated after Susan Morrison. It must be this John Morrison about whose circumstances in October, 1864, the *Official Records of the Union and Confederate Navies* refer. Three boats, two officers, and 30 men commanded by Unionist Captain Gillespie sailed up the White Oak Creek destined for the Morrison Plantation where corn, harvested by the Morrison people, was being distributed to destitute Confederates. On October 14, 1864 Gillespie returned to the vessel awaiting him in St. Andrew's Sound, and in tow were 47 Africans who had been taken from the Morrison Plantation.

In 1998, St. Simons businessman Jasper Barnes wonders whether his maternal Morrison ancestors came on the Island by this transport and after freedom took the surname of a former Morrison master.

# Georgia's Hofwyl-Broadfield Plantation

*Photograph by Ed Mathews*

Step back in time and contemplate the wonder of the natural world in an unsurpassed setting. From the veranda of the Dent's plantation plain-style farm house (ca. 1850), allow your senses to feast on the hauntingly beautiful surroundings. Ancient, hoary live oaks *(Quercus virginiana)*, named for the Misses Dent, Miriam and Ophelia, frame their former home.

Gazing out over a high bluff and past the century-old magnolias which flank the front porch, imagine a different world! In the 1770s, a Quaker naturalist Will Bartram trekked through the delta lands, and he likely listened to the cacophony of native ivory-bill woodpeckers. Thick cypress swamps festooned with lush Spanish moss *(Tillandsia usenoides)* must have presented a spellbinding, ethereal view to Bartram's eyes.

But by the late 18th century, Carolina rice-growers who had exhausted fertile soils, pushed into the tidewater reaches of coastal Georgia. North to South, only five rivers--the Savannah, Ogeechee, Altamaha, Satilla, and St. Mary's Rivers, were suitable for rice culti-vation. Gambler's choice for lucrative profits, after substantial invest-ments.

On the backs of Africans captured along the Gold Coast, rice planters built their fortunes and amassed the trappings of great wealth. The "Gullahs" (possibly after "Angola") brought with them the knowledge and skills necessary to cultivate and nurture a delicious, healthful grain. Tools, such as the *daba* (small hoe), flail-stick, and mortar and pestle, fashioned from pine and cypress were critical for processing rice. Even today, rice-fanning baskets produced from pine needles and sweet grass *(Muhlenbergia)* influence the coastal decorative arts, compliments of Sapelo's famed Allen Green, master basketmaker.

Plantation work and play songs, perpetuated by the elders were passed along to youth. Imagine the workers returning from the rice fields, singing. Shout songs, "Oh Eve--where is Adam" reflect the complexity of chants preserved by musicologist Lydia Parrish. Surely she visited on the Dent plantation and talked with the freedmen and women who lingered on near the beloved plantation.

Did they tell her about the unhealthy malarial swamps where the "miasma" raged, killing scores? Africans who benefited from a distinct genetic trait possessed an immunity to the ravages of malaria. Because of these seasonal fevers, coastal rice growers, as absentee owners, often abandoned their tidewater plantations in the Spring, Summer and Fall months.

Resort living on Cumberland Island, at the Mineral Springs in Waynesville (present-day Brantley County), or in fashionable cities, such as Savannah and Charleston, South Carolina, offered respite for the planters' families. Overseers ran the business of the working rice plantation during their long absences.

Hollywood's depiction of mint juleps, cultured southern gentlemen and hoop-skirted belles, magnolias and magnificent plantation homes had no basis for reality in Georgia's testy rice country. What did survive were "Africanisms" prolonged under conditions of extreme isolation. The old coastal society included the aristocracy of the "Rice Culture." Men such as the erudite James Hamilton Couper of Hopeton; planter genius Hugh Fraser Grant of Elizafield, Evelyn and Grantley Plantations, Philadelphian Pierce Mease Butler of Butler Island and Hampton, and the Brailsford-Troup-Dent family of Broadfield, later Hofwyl-Broadfield.

As she wandered through her comfortable home, "Miss Ophelia" surely contemplated the sorrow, happiness and joy that emanated from an old house. She certainly treasured the legacy of five generations living on the "Broadface" tract, and at Broughton Island, described by her grandmother as "Golgotha" or the hill of skulls after the loss of human life from a severe hurricane.

At her death on September 5, 1973 "Miss Ophelia" willed much of her worldly goods to the Nature Conservancy, which conveyed the property, including 1,268 acres to the Department of Natural Resources. As a golden apple Miss Mary McGarvey eloquently wrote, "The land she could not leave to the horror of urban sprawl and smear. She wanted it kept as an oasis for future generations."

Three years after her death, a bicentennial project titled "Man in the Landscape" was held in Darien. In the handsome publication produced in conjunction with this two-day conference, editor William G. "Bill" Haynes, Jr. included a letter written by Miss Dent.

"I am convinced it (rice growing) will return to these parts in the not too distant future because of the steady lowering of the middle west water shed for the most part, and also because of the great need of producing more food for the increasing population.... I beg you to look carefully into these angles--ecology, pollution, spawning grounds and potential food crops, before going ahead with the development of the Altamaha River."

# Freedman's Rest

In recent memory, the old people of Harrington, Southend and Jewtown, of Brookman, Needwood and Petersville frequently referred to a time "before freedom." No stigma was attached--the term was simply a point of reference in the course of a privileged afternoon conversation. Shared hours which enriched my life. But as time goes by, fewer coastal residents comprehend that expression, "before freedom."

Sprawling over an antebellum coastal landscape, large-scale rice and cotton plantations once acquired a reputation for the quality of their staples. And for a sumptuous living. On the back of Africans, these planters built their fame and fortune; their names live on.

But many Africans were noted for their expertise. At the John Couper plantation on Cannon's Point, chef Sans Foix was hailed for his culinary abilities and fabulous dishes. On Sapelo, Mohammaden Bullali remembered his north African ancestry by composing a mysterious diary. We know now that "Bullali's diary" was a palimpsest, a mnemonic device used to recall religious tenets.

After freedom, there was Uncle Liverpool Hazzard, who acquired considerable business savvy from life at Butler's Island, a spreading rice plantation on the delta of the great Altamaha River. Hazzard eventually opened a "slave museum" in his home in Darien. And charged admission.

After freedom, there were Shad Hall and "Miss Katie" Brown of Sapelo Island, widely known as story-tellers, about life "before freedom."

It is good and it is important that these people be remembered. Have you ever heard of "Freedman's Rest," a settlement once located in the northeastern corner of Glynn County, but now obscured by the necessities of a coastal military presence? The Glynco Naval Air Station was erected at the outset of World War II to combat the German submarine menace offshore. Squarely in the path of this planned airbase lay the Freedman's Rest community, the Freedman's Rest Missionary Baptist Church and a cemetery.

In February 1866, George C. Dent drew up articles of agreement for the signature of freedmen who were hired for the purpose of cultivating the rice plantation known as Hofwyl. Dent offered to furnish rent-free homes for the workers and their families and to provide provisions whose cost was to be deducted from their portion of the crop sales. Morever, the agreement stipulated that the plantation was to be worked as formerly and that the laborers must assume responsibility for the care and maintenance of "all tools and equipment of husbandry" which Dent would issue them. He would share the cost of rice seed with the freedmen but he would expect them to work cheerfully, obeying all orders. Dent pledged "to treat them kindly, and to try to work in harmony for the benefit of both parties."

In time, numerous families 'founded' and settled in Freedman's Rest: the Jacksons, the Capers, the Magwoods, the Haines, the Ormonds. A Missionary Baptist Church grew there. In 1912, the trustees of the Church sold a strip of land 35 feet in width right through the settlement to the Georgia Coast and Piedmont Railroad.

Eloise Polite remembers this: walking with her grandmother Catherine Jackson Keith every second Sunday from Needwood to services held in Freedman's Rest by the Reverend L.T. Tison or the Reverend Curry of McIntosh County.

As for the cemetery, when the Navy arrived, negotiations got underway and the result was the removal of that sacred plot to a site off the Petersville Road. There they are now: Sullivans, Polites, Rogers, Pittmans and more. The oldest marker dated 1910. Ruth Gamble Sullivan is buried there; she died at age 22 in 1941. Her daughter is Frankie Sullivan Quimby, lead vocalist for the Sea Island Singers.

# Images of the Plantation Mistress

In 1982, a Yankee gal named Catherine Clinton published a book entitled *The Plantation Mistress* in which she raised important questions about the social history of "the Lost Cause." She especially commented on the scholarly neglect suffered by the plantation mistress and observed that her role was a critical one in plantation management.

Clinton determined that endless duties and responsibilities, health and disease factors weighed upon the shoulders and daily affairs of this long suffering soul. But in a patriarchal world, the shadowy presence of a woman--the plantation mistress--paled when compared with chivalrous cavaliers and prosperous planters.

The financial basis for a planter-dominated society turned upon large-scale cultivation of certain staple crops: corn, cotton, rice, sugar cane, indigo. Driven by the demands of world markets, these crops not only enslaved the Africans brought over to cultivate them, but the plantation mistress as well. Catherine Clinton argues that this woman was "the slave of slaves."

Here are brief portraits of three coastal Georgia women of that era. First, Isabella Maria Hazzard who, in 1793, married General John Floyd in Beaufort, South Carolina.They soon settled on Bellevue Plantation at Floyd's Neck, Camden County, Georgia where they grew cotton, indigo, rice and white mulberries. The Floyds reserved two hundred acres for a military parade ground and the training of a coastal militia. In time, they cleared a live oak and cedar lined mile roadway between Bellevue and their other farm, Fairfield. By 1825, the Floyds had completed a grand manor house, anchor-shaped, in tribute to their participation in the coastal trade.

The foundation of this remarkable building was made of eight foot tabby walls rising to a cypress upper story. Piazzas supported by columns faced spacious lawns, a vineyard and an orchard. A semi-circular drawing room framed the view of Mrs. Floyd's formal rose garden. Flowering trees, shrubs and bulbs were imported from the Caribbean to enhance the Floyd's interest in outdoor recreation. Southern hospitality assumed new dimensions with the arrival of The Camden Hunting Club which brought together other coastal planter families.

Anna Matilda Page married Thomas Butler King at Retreat Plantation on St. Simons Island on December 2, 1824; the ceremony was conducted by the Reverend Edmund Matthews of Christ Episcopal

Church. A Massachusetts native, King quickly adapted to the graciousness of plantation life and the management of his wife's inherited property which soon included large holdings near Waverly, Camden County. But the Kings made their lasting mark at Retreat, overlooking St. Simons Sound and Jekyll Island. Retreat's long-staple cotton was recognized on the world market for its quality and value as a cash crop.

The four-storied cotton house on the property proved a beacon for mariners, many of whom brought shrubs and bulbs to thrive in Anna Matilda's formal gardens. Ninety-five varieties of roses were grown in a horse-shoe shape, bordered by hedges of crepe myrtle and oleander. A kitchen garden provided thyme and other flavorful spices and herbs for seasoning the bounty of coastal cuisine.

During their thirty-five years of marriage, and across King's frequent absences due to political and business affairs, Anna Matilda and her ten children prospered. Retreat gained a reputation for gracious living and hospitality which won over numerous international guests. John James Audubon visited there and the estate prompted the great ornithologist to fancy a "fairy island" of another golden age.

Revolutionary Loyalist, Captain Alexander Campbell Wylly and his bride, Margaret Armstrong eventually returned to coastal Georgia and settled in their "Village Plantation" on St. Simons Island. On Christmas Day, 1827, their sixteen year old daughter, Caroline, married James Hamilton Couper in a ceremony held in the Wylly's drawing room. The couple then departed for their Hopeton Plantation home located near the ricefields of the south branch of the Altamaha River. James Hamilton Couper's reputation for plantation management was admired and copied by other planters. Gracious gardens bordered the ricefields. Cypress dugouts were raced in regattas on the waterways. The Coupers hosted artists and scholars such as Sir Charles Lyell, the great genius of geological sciences.

Here then are three plantation mistresses: Isabella Maria Hazzard Floyd--Anna Matilda Page King--Caroline Wylly Couper! Burnette Vanstory in her book *Georgia's Land of the Golden Isles* remarks on the arrival of such women. "Into new land they brought old traditions, old customs, plants and cuttings from old gardens, old recipes, old wine." Ancestral mahogany and other fine woods gave shape to stately homes. Oil paintings, large libraries, silverware and serving pieces and Chinese export porcelain suggest great wealth. All of this presided over by the wives and mothers, the plantation mistress of an antebellum south.

# An "Obligation Pond" at the Harrington Community on St. Simons Island

"Harrington Hall" was the 500 acre plantation owned by Raymond Demere, one of Oglethorpe's officers. There is a marker erected by the State of Georgia on Lawrence Road which establishes the approximate location of the estate. The exact location has not yet been determined by archaeological excavation but the prospect is that the site would yield material debris associated with early 18th century France and England.

Near the marker is another "Harrington" community, this one comprised of descendants of African slaves and dating from the Reconstruction era. The family names here: Ramsey, Whing, Davis, Sullivan, Hunter, the population of a once traditional black community.

Few of the "old people" who passed along ancient African oral histories remain to tell the young folks about times past and the richness of their ways. Few of the present day residents know about the importance of a pond of water in yesteryear's rites of passage, baptismal rites.

Harrington resident Neptune Whing shares his memories of "Obligation Pond," having been raised near this spring-fed one acre three feet deep freshwater pond. Red maples thrived there. Across the way, for many years, stood the Henry Whing family home though it is long fallen down.

Neptune heard of Obligation Pond from his grandmother Mrs. Catherine McIver Whing. Plantation workers used it for baptism. "They talked about something strange about that pond. A couple was riding in a buggy and possibly their horse spooked and they rode into the pond and disappeared."

Is this anecdote the descendant of an older tale? African priests were among those snatched by slavers and transported to the American colonies to work on the large cotton, rice, corn and indigo plantations. They, too, "disappeared into the water." Later they easily blended their earlier traditions with Christian beliefs.

For that matter, Charles and Emma Hunter of the Harrington community recall Grandmother Louise telling of Bahamian ancestors who may have been a source of the river baptisms "which were later held by members of the local churches." The ceremonies were conducted on the ebb tide which long ago, it was believed, carried one's sins away.

Scholars have long been interested in such ritual. Margaret Davis Cate has used the reminiscences of the "old people" in two notable volumes: *Our Todays and Yesterdays* and *Early Days of Coastal Georgia.* "On either side of Frederica Road and within the settlement known as Harrington---it is called Obligation Pond for here they took their obligation to the Lord."

Lydia Parrish's *Slave Songs of the Georgia Sea Islands* is a work of great love and devotion to dying traditions, inspired by "Miss Julia" and Joe Armstrong of Southend.

The old Harrington neighborhood is nicely represented in the classic WPA book *Drums and Shadows: Survival Studies Among the Georgia Coastal Negroes.*

# The Wylly-Couper Alliance and a Christmas Wedding Dress

*Photo courtesy of The Coastal Georgia Historical Society*

Young Mary Houstoun and her sister, Eliza, of Marengo Plantation in McIntosh County visited with the Wylly family of St. Simons Island for several days prior to a very special wedding. On December 22, 1827, Mary wrote her mother that they had lunched at Doboy with the Yonge family and experienced a "safe and pleasant trip from Marengo to Cousin Margaret's delightful Island home."

Mary Houstoun's "Wylly Letters" are detailed descriptions of the coastal terrain and of the customs, habits and circumstances of early 19th century plantation families in Glynn and McIntosh counties.

Revolutionary Loyalists, the Wylly brothers, William and Alexander, had fled to the Bahamas where Alexander married Margaret Armstrong. In time Alexander Wylly settled on St. Simons Island on land formerly occupied by a community of German Lutherans who had themselves arrived in the previous century. (A state historic marker presently identifies the site of "the German village.")

So it was that Mary Houstoun came to the Island in 1827 to witness the wedding of Caroline Wylly and James Hamilton Couper of Hopeton and Hamilton plantations. The Christmas ceremony, Reverend Edmund Matthews of Christ Episcopal Church presiding, was held that evening in the Wylly drawing room. "The lawn was lit by four fire stands and it was very picturesque." Thereafter, the bride and groom departed for their home at Hopeton, located in the rice fields in the delta of the south branch of the Altamaha River.

"Caroline is an almost perfectly beautiful girl. She was very sweet in manner to us both."

Writing to her mother two days later, Mary described the sixteen year old bride's wedding dress made by Madam Beaulard of Congress Street in Savannah. "The wedding dress is of crepe de lisse over a white satin slip. The corsage full and rather high in front edged with a narrow rouleau of lace. The sleeves are very short, puffed full, and set in a satin band, giving the effect of the calyx of a flower. The skirt has two rows of graduated satin leaves arranged in two rows from the hem to the waist. In front the waist is finished with a satin sash." It was a gown fit for a young woman, a plantation mistress whose home would in time receive such dignitaries as Sir Charles Lyell, the geologist and Swedish abolitionist Frederika Bremer.

# Living in
the Past

# Of the Tree Brought from Florida, Which is Called Sassafras

Historian "Miss Mamie" Ross made a fascinating comment in a valuable booklet, *Spanish Days in Glynn County*. "Interest in sassafras gathering initiated the earliest development of Glynn County, for the influx of inquisitive foreign intruders to her Georgia lands brought Spain into action." Earliest development based on the gathering of sassafras?

What does the historic record say about the lowly sassafras as a coveted New World commodity? What role did famous adventurers, botanists and surgeons play in its export? What is the "Cumberland connection" between the southernmost of Georgia's coastal sea islands and sassafras? To answer these questions, we must ponder the "golden age of herbs and herbalists," four centuries ago.

The Renaissance was the great age of the discovery, exploration, and settlement in the New World. North America became a 'field of conquest' for the European powers of England, France and Spain. Early Spanish excursions were followed by a temporary French settlement, most notably in 1562 at "Charlesfort," near present-day Parris Island, South Carolina.

In May, 1563, a London printer published an important report titled *The Whole and True Discoverie of Terra Florida*. Written by the famed French corsair Jean Ribaut, this English version of his narrative purported "to make a true reporte"in which he told about the temperature, fertility, ports, havens, rivers and generally all the commodities found in that land, and about the conditions and customs of the natives.

Ribaut urged the reigning French monarch, Charles IX to continue and diligently follow French settlement in North America. Between 1562-1565, "La Caroline," the French Huguenot colony at Fort Caroline on the St. John's River near present-day Jacksonville, Florida, realized Ribaut's short-lived vision.

To checkmate French designs, the Spanish initiated a program of presidios, fortifications and missions in "la Florida." On September 8, 1565, Captain-General Pedro Menendez de Aviles established San Agustin, as the "first permanent Spanish settlement in North

America." Vaguely defined, "la Florida" included all the territory between the current boundaries of South Carolina on the north, west to the Mississippi River, south to the Florida Straits, and bounded on the east by the Atlantic Ocean.

Upon their return to Europe, the French had reported being sickly due to "grievous and variable diseases," throughout their Florida travels. Indians known as the Timucuan showed them a medicinal tree, the manner in which to use it and to heal their many ills. The Europeans called the tree sassafras; the Indians called it *pauame*.

Ultimately, a famous physician of Seville, Dr. Nicholas Monardes deserves credit for the promotion of the beneficial aspects of sassafras. On October 1, 1577 an enterprising London merchant, Thomas Frampton, translated and printed Monardes' book *Joyful News out of the Newfound World*. Eager to promote New World botany, Monardes spared few details in his praise of the "marvelous effects" of sassafras "on diverse and sundry diseases." This panacea proved especially useful to comfort the liver, the stomach, the kidneys, to restore appetite and in treatment of the gout. Monardes reported that Pedro Menendez and his men had prepared a sassafras tea to treat the fevers and agues with which they were afflicted.

In preparation, Monardes advised that the "wood and roote" of the tree be cut into small, thin pieces and boiled to an unspecified consistency. He described the sweet smell of sassafras rind, similar to fennel, with much sweetness of taste. Its sharpness in color and taste and pleasantness in smell were similar to cinnamon. The tree grew near the sea in temperate places.

In December 1597, the barber-surgeon John Gerard published *The Herbal or General History of Plants*. Although his work lacked originality, Gerard based it on the respected Latin herbal of 1583 by Dodoens. Unrivaled for over two decades and with imperfections, *Gerard's* was England's guide. It remains to this day a "lasting monument of Renaissance botany." Gerard recorded that "the sassafras tree grows very much like the Pine tree, the trunk or body is straight, smooth, and void of boughs, of a great height... This tree grows in most parts of the West Indies, especially about the cape of Florida." The "ague tree" possessed a reputation for curing fevers. Gerard specified that the root worked the best effect, especially if the color of the rind were tawny. He advised that the wood be cut into small pieces and boiled to the color of claret wine.

American Indian medicine demonstrates a long tradition of sassafras use by the natives. Alternately, a contemporary account in *The Foxfire Book* celebrates the wisdom of north Georgia Appalachian mountain folk who prepared sassafras tea as a "blood builder." Curiously, the Emmaus, Pennsylvania Rodale Company's *Illustrated Encyclopedia of Herbs*, stated that sassafras has fallen into disfavor. Although once valued as a flavoring agent, for instance, in "root beer," its volatile oil, safrole, has been identified as a carcinogen. The federal USDA outlawed the sales of flavorings that contain sassafras.

Today, this native deciduous tree is a neglected one in the ornamental landscape. A small tree that reaches 20-40 feet in height, sassafras is a member of the laurel family. It may be easily recognized in the wild because of its spicy-aromatic fragrance, brilliant green and characteristic mitten-shaped leaves; its leaves feature a splash of yellow and red Fall color. Cumberland is the largest of Georgia's fabled "golden isles." Many people recognize the various names assigned to this beautiful island, including Tacatacuru, Ile de la Seine, and San Pedro. Less well known are the terms "Missoe" or "Wissoe," which mean "sassafras." Cumberland Island--the island of sassafras, the lowly sassafras.

# Southeastern Indians and a Useful Plant Called Smilax

Spring spurt surrounds us everywhere in the beautiful Golden Isles, the fantasia of various colored azaleas, dogwood and wisteria blanket the landscape and the fragrance of the lovely tea olive scents the air. Creeping in their midst and through the English ivy is a clinging woody vine called Smilax, commonly known as "greenbrier, cat brier, or China root."

Its presence in the ornamental landscape is a bane to many gardeners. The U.S. Department of Agriculture lists Smilax as a weed, or plant out of place. Those who have tried to eradicate it discover that the underground stem tubers of the woody smilaxes promote survival! Among the wild food plants used by the Indians of the Southeastern United States several species of Smilax were clearly important. The 18th century Quaker naturalist, Will Bartram, for example, noted that "a species of Smilax afford the Indians a delicious and nourishing food, which is prepared from its vast, tuberous roots."

Who were the Indians of the Southeast? What type of plant is Smilax? And as a food source, how did the native Southeastern Indians use this ubiquitous and persistent woody vine?

The Southeastern Indians were those socially diverse, yet cultural-
ly similar, indigenous inhabitants of the American South. Their geographical boundaries were demarcated on the East by the Atlantic
Ocean, on the South by the Gulf of Mexico, on the West by the aridity
of east Texas, and on the North by the cold, upper reaches of the
Mississippi and Ohio River valleys. Approximately three-fourths of
the Southeastern Cultural Area lay in the Coastal Plain, a biotic
province which enjoys a temperate climate, lush vegetation, and
which once contained an abundance of game animals.

Our historic amnesia about the presence of Southeastern Indians
largely stems from their forced "removal" to Indian territory, or
Oklahoma during the 1830s. Yet curiously, along the Georgia coast
ample evidence still exists for their long ago presence, especially in
the Archaic period shell middens and sand mounds. But until recently,
knowledge about the Southeastern Indians has been the occupation of
anthropologists or archaeologists and a very specialized field
called ethnobotany focuses on the use of plants by man.

The generic term "Smilax" derives from an ancient Greek word for
an evergreen oak. Smilax is a genus of the *Liliaceae* or lily family,
comprising about 250 species, which are most abundant in the temperate tropical zones of the Americas and Asia; in the Southeast, the
temperate zone is the focus of Smilax distribution. As a natural food
source, our concern is with the woody species of Smilax, nine of
which thrive in the Southeast.

Because tubers preserve so poorly, the archaeological record yields
scant evidence of Smilax exploitation. The Newt Kash Rock Shelter is
the oldest archaeological evidence of this woody tuber. Initially, the
prehistoric inhabitants of this rock shelter were dated from the
Archaic Tradition, estimated at 4,000 years ago, but may have been
Woodland Indians.

Historical accounts provide a rich source of information on the use
of Smilax by Indians. Especially important are the 18th century
colonial accounts of early travelers, traders and statesmen. In North
Carolina, John Lawson noted that the Carolina Indians boiled the
roots and ate them; they also hardened the fibrous roots and used
them to make ornamental heads for walking canes.

James Adair, who lived and traded among the Indians from 1735
until 1768, furnishes a wealth of information. Adair observed, "It is
surprising to see the great variety of dishes they make out of wild

flesh, corn, beans, peas, potatoes, pompions, dried fruits, herbs and roots."

When the Indians on St. Catherine's Island served him the tender shoots of the China brier, it reminded James Oglethorpe of asparagus. This is not surprising, since both Smilax and Asparagus are members of the lily family. Today, naturalists prepare and serve the delicious tender shoots of Smilax, a source of vitamin C, in a similar fashion as asparagus.

Perhaps the most intriguing, and clearly, the most complete accounts of Smilax processing and use, come from the pen of the Quaker naturalist Will Bartram. His well-known travels through the Southeast occurred from 1773 until 1777. Bartram recorded in his field journals descriptions of the fauna and flora, some of which are now extinct, as well as the beliefs, customs, and habits of the Southeastern Indians.

William Bartram and company were entertained in one instance by the "White King" at a farewell dinner, which proved to be a sumptuous Indian banquet. They feasted at Talahasochte, a Seminole town which was situated on the Suwannee River in Levy County, Florida.

In his *Travels*, Bartram noted "There was a noble entertainment and repast provided against our arrival, consisting of bears ribs, venison, varieties of fish, roasted turkeys, hot corn cakes, and a very agreeable, cooling sort of jelly, which they call *conte*; this is prepared from the root of the China brier."

Red *conte* flour, says Bartram, was mixed with warm water and sweetened with honey or sugar to yield "a beautiful, delicious jelly, very nourishing and wholesome." This nutritious jelly was frequently eaten by infants and the toothless old people. Also, the *conte* meal, blended with fine corn flour, and fried in fresh bear's oil, produced hot cakes or fritters.

In south Florida, the Seminoles processed the starchy roots of *Zamia integrifolia*, a native cycad, to produce white *coontie/kunti*. This change in their subsistence strategy may be attributed to the abundance of the Zamia plant and the dwindling occurrence of Smilax species. But in our time, the Zamia is an endangered species due to the impact of development on its habitat.

Finally, historian J. Leitch Wright, Jr. discussed the importance of maize (corn) and tobacco to the Southeastern Muscogulges (Creek/Seminoles). He noted that "Of the two, maize was of the most

consequence for the southeastern Indians because it was their principal food and it played a significant role in their religion." He states
that maize replaced Indian reliance upon the starchy roots of Zamia
and Smilax when this tasseled plant was introduced into the Southeast
from Mesoamerica.

This suggests that the use of Smilax played an important role in
the subsistence strategy of the Indians of the Southeast for millennia.
Smilax--the China brier and a tenacious clinging woody vine may
have been crucial to other aspects of the culture of the native
Southeastern Indians.

# Edmund Gray

Frontier circumstances attract stalwart settlers who brave uncertain conditions. But the call of the wild also draws pirates, rogues, ruffians, adventurers and opportunists. These colorful figures give spice to the pages of our coastal history and lore. For instance, where did Edward Teach, the notorious Blackbeard, bury his treasure?

Such rascals provide a yardstick by which to measure civilized behavior. Ponder the activities of an 18th century fellow named Edmund Gray. A Virginia Quaker, Gray moved to Georgia about 1750 and established a "shadow government" at Brandon, near Augusta. His involvement in politics straddled a transition period from when Georgia was a proprietary colony, administered by a Trustees board, to government by royal appointment. Gray's confrontational behavior and his inclination to trade with the Indians were sources of great concern to three royal governors: John Reynolds and Henry Ellis of Georgia and William Lyttelton of South Carolina.

Elected to serve as one of the nineteen representatives in Georgia's legislative branch called the Commons House of Assembly, Gray represented the interests of Augusta. Several of his cronies, Charles Watson of Savannah among them, also won election to the new assembly. Gray and his followers soon became a threat to the orderly function of the Assembly. They deliberately absented themselves in order to prevent a quorum; moreover they signed a letter considered seditious by both the Commons and the Upper House. Expelled in January, 1755, Gray and his men moved south of the Altamaha River into neutral territory.

On February 28, 1755, Governor Reynolds wrote the Board of Trade that Gray had "an artful way of instilling jealousy of their liberties into the peoples minds." He added, perhaps unnecessarily, Gray lacked scruples. Gray's was a "lawless crew who lived like Indians by hunting only." They created apprehension among the planters.

Some twenty families followed Edmund Gray thirty miles up the tidal flow of the "Great Satilly River" where they created a settlement which they called New Hanover. They quickly devised rules of government allowing for land allotment and taxation to build and maintain a fort. A board of commissioners regulated the sale of cattle and tree cutting.

However, New Hanover was perceived by the Crown as being in

clear violation of royal land-grant policies. As subjects of England, their presence in this ill-defined territory compromised peace which had been established in 1748 by the Treaty of Aix-la-Chapelle between England and Spain.

In October, 1757, the Governor of Spanish Florida complained to Governor Henry Ellis and requested the removal of Gray's Gang from His Catholic Majesty's Territories. Because of such threats, Gray and about two-thirds of his followers moved to Cumberland Island where they continued to engage in trade with both the Spanish and the Creek Indians.

South Carolina's lingering claim to this neutral territory resulted in Governor Lyttelton's insistence, joined with that of Governor Ellis, that New Hanover be evacuated.

Subsequently two commissioners, James Edward Powell of Georgia and Major Henry Hyme of South Carolina, went to the Satilla settlement to post a public notice of eviction. Then, they returned to Cumberland for a similar purpose.

Powell's report provides insight into the circumstances at New Hanover when they arrived on the first day of February, 1759. "We were kindly received by the principal settlers and very much pleased to find their dispositions better than had been represented." They very submissively agreed to abandon New Hanover. Powell and Hyme collected and recorded the names of household heads. (A boon for present-day genealogists!)

Finally in March, 1759, Thomas Goldsmith, commanding His Majesty's Independent Company of Foot at Fort Frederica, following a visit to New Hanover and Cumberland, reported that the former had been abandoned and that on the Island "where the major part of these people did formerly reside," there was but one man. This fellow had been left behind in their haste to abandon Cumberland Island. The settlers "had not time to carry off" their possessions and so he served the purpose of caring for their worldly goods and tending the abundant fields of rye.

You will not find a marker to designate the site of Gray's New Hanover colony. There was one, and it stood near the Satilla where "Burnt Fort" was, but the marker was taken away for repair and never returned.

# A Bicentennial Event and
# the Treaty of Coleraine

*Photo by the author*

Bicentennial events capture the popular imagination and provide an opportunity for celebrating coastal Georgia's rich history. In support of "heritage roots" these community gatherings enrich our lives and re-enforce a strong 'sense of place' traditional to the customs in the American South.

For instance, in July, 1936 local citizenry commemorated the founding of Fort Frederica with a three-day extravaganza, sponsored by the newly formed Glynn County Historic Landmarks Commission. Few today will argue the importance of preserving Frederica or its critical spot on the late 20th century's coastal tourism map. But are you aware of the bicentennial of an important Indian treaty that occurred on June 29, 1796? Called the "Treaty of Peace and Friendship" held at Coleraine, an old town located in the southwest corner of Camden County, its implications were far reaching. And even a patriotic organization honored the Treaty of Coleraine. In April, 1912 the Lyman Hall Chapter of the Daughters of the American Revolution (DAR) erected an impressive limestone boulder whose marble plaque recognizes this important treaty. At Coleraine, it stands today on the private retreat of the Varn family, near a lovely spot along a lazing St. Mary's River.

Recently, the name "Coleraine" received wide currency when the city commission of Kingsland changed the road name within the city limits to Laurel Island Parkway. Responding to this act, many coastal Georgians expressed outrage and disbelief that county and city officials were unaware of the antiquity and historic importance of this old, old route.

What happened at Coleraine and why is it significant in Georgia history? First, let's clarify the widespread "myth" that the Coleraine Treaty was "one of the few treaties recorded in which the Indians did not lose land." In fact, the treaty signing by about 400 mostly Upper Creek Indians reaffirmed and made obligatory on the contracting parties a boundary line.

Negotiated at the Treaty of New York, signed on August 7, 1790 with the Creek Indians, the cession of the coveted "Oconee Indian lands" included about three million acres of land, lying between the Ogeechee and Oconee Rivers. As Georgians pushed into these frontier territories, little did they contemplate the richness of the Southeastern Indian's "world view."

In simple terms, two conflicting cultures struggled over food and territory, and as the 18th century progressed, native peoples had become dependent upon exotic "trade goods." For instance, shiny hatchets, guns and bullets, red and blue trade cloth, woolen blankets, trade beads and trinkets caught their eye, and irretrievably changed the subsistence needs of the Indians of the Southeast.

In Spanish Florida, the Scottish firm of Panton, Leslie and Company, headquartered at Pensacola and Mobile, capitalized upon this dependency and further exploited a centuries' old pelt and hide trade. Meanwhile, a fledgling federal government led by President

George Washington sought to stabilize Creek-American relations. On April 18, 1796, Congress established a factory system whose intent was to set up government trading factories, or posts "to trade fairly with the Indians," and this system lasted until 1822.

Located at an important "cultural crossroads" Coleraine's role featured the bustling trading post, which was swept up in frontier intrigue. Edward Price served as factor, Lieutenant Col. Henry Gaither commanded a garrison of federal troops, and James Seagrove served as agent to the Creek Indians at Coleraine. Georgians were anxious to push into the territory between the Altamaha and St. Mary's Rivers, a no-man's-land, and state officials resented the interference of federal authorities in their treatment of the native Southeastern Indians.

Claiming sole authority to negotiate treaties with the Indians, the federal government appointed North Carolinian Benjamin Hawkins, George Clymer of Pennsylvania and Andrew Pickens of South Carolina as commissioners to negotiate the Treaty of Coleraine. Accompanied by militiamen, Georgia's delegation included James Hendricks, James Jackson later governor of Georgia, and James Simms.

Federal interpreters included Timothy Barnard, Alexander Cornells, James Burges and Langley Bryant. To this group, the Georgians added Philip Scott, and the esteemed Indian spokesman, Fusatchee Mico, or White-Bird King. At Coleraine, the conference opened on June 16 and lasted until the treaty signing on June 29, 1796 when ten articles cemented the agreements.

Afterwards, an uneasy peace ensued; frontier Georgians resented the intrusion of government into Georgia's insatiable quest for an expanded territory, and states' rights. In fact, a Chatham County Superior Court expressed the opinion that the federal Commissioners had usurped the powers "to make rules and regulations for the citizens of this state, during the late treaty at Coleraine."

# Cemeteries Found,
# Cemeteries Lost Forever

Old roads in Brantley, Camden and Glynn Counties have been fair
game for me in search of rural and often "forgotten" cemeteries and
family "roots." For over two years, Mother and I searched along the
old Post Road for the Burney family cemetery, located on a large 19th
century ante-bellum plantation. The "wiregrass" genealogist Judge
Folks Huxford had noted that the William Burney homeplace was the
final resting spot of our maternal ancestor, James Stafford. Stafford
had married Elizabeth Burney on June 5, 1845; he served a short term
as high sheriff in 1832 and later served two terms in 1837 and 1845 as
a state representative from Wayne County.

Mother and I thoroughly enjoyed our adventures on the back roads
of southeast Georgia! We re-discovered old friends and relatives,
made new friends and met kind strangers. Also, we located the
Stafford burial ground at Whitaker Hill, found the Mt. Olive
Cemetery, and near Tarboro, finally visited the Bickley Chapel and its
small cemetery that my Mother's brother told us about in so many of
his tall tales.

In spite of maps, plats and the assistance of kindly friends, we
never could locate the "old Burney family cemetery," along the Post
Road. This gnawed at me and my questions never ceased. Finally, an
oldtimer said, "You never will find James Stafford and the Burney
family plots!" Spell-bound I sat and listened as he told me the story of
how the cemetery had been destroyed in the late 1940s or early 1950s
by a man of questionable humanity. Never will I understand why this
man destroyed the resting place of my ancestors! Willful and wanton
destruction of a private family cemetery? Did the Burney family
"except" or reserve the use of the family cemetery when title passed
to another?*

My resolution was to learn more about the preservation and protection of cemeteries and the laws and statutes that provide for "the
common wish of mankind to insure a fitting resting place for the
dead." One of the ways that I could learn about cemetery law was by
talking with someone who had been involved in the direct application
of preservation statutes. Immediately, Mrs. Mattie Gladstone came to

mind. So, one fair and windy day we met at the newly constructed Darien waterfront dockage and talked about her experiences at Sidon Plantation and the Western Dunwody Cemetery, along the old River Road.

Mrs. Gladstone's volunteer and archaeological recovery work have familiarized her with the terrain and material objects associated with James Smith's tidewater rice plantation called Sidon. Situated on Cathead Creek and slated for commercial development, this Altamaha River valley plantation once boasted 2,300 acres of land in rice and pinelands. Connected with the plantation was Dunwody Cemetery where an undetermined number of white and black gravesites have been lost due to developmental pressures. Today, the lone tombstone of Rebecca West stands in testament of her memory and "dead but not forgotten." Because of her interests in history and archaeology, Mrs. Gladstone not only serves a second term as president of the Lower Altamaha Historical Society (LAHS), but also has been very active in the affairs of the Cemetery Committee. Sponsored by the historical group, the purpose of the Cemetery Committee is to locate and document all burial grounds, county-wide. According to Mrs. Gladstone, "Part of the comprehensive plan for McIntosh County as recommended by the regional development center (RDC) was to locate and document cemeteries and the presence of human remains. So far, we have now identified 69 cemeteries, excluding Indian burial sites."

Familiarity with House Bill #402 which became effective on April 11, 1991 has empowered Mrs. Gladstone to speak effectively about Georgia's preservation statutes pertaining to the "protection and preservation of certain cemeteries." When we talked about the circumstances at the Western Dunwody Cemetery, Mrs. Gladstone commented "It is gratifying to see that the present owners are complying with the law."

Highlights of House Bill #402 regarding the protection/preservation of certain cemeteries and their removal include in section 3, "...The General Assembly declares that human remains and burial objects are not property to be owned by the person who owns the land or water where the human remains or burial objects are discovered. Such remains and burial objects are part of the finite, unrenewable cultural heritage of the people of Georgia." And, "No owner or occupier of land shall knowingly disturb burial grounds, cemeteries, human remains, or burial objects thereon unless the owner or occupier first obtains a permit from the governing authority of the municipality or county where the cemetery or burial ground is located." Also, "If a person knowingly fails to comply with this Chapter, he shall be guilty of a misdemeanor of a high and aggravated nature, and upon conviction, shall be fined not more than $5,000 for each grave site disturbed. A person convicted under owner's disturbance of cemetery for the purpose of developing or changing the use of the land without a permit shall be incarcerated for not more than six months and shall be fined not less than $5,000 for each grave site disturbed."

*In late 1997, I learned that the Burney Cemetery was located near Hopewell Church. In fact, the encroaching pine forest loosely defines the Burney-Popwell Cemetery, popularly known as the Popwell Cemetery today. Moreover, I've come on an old map which designates the grave of an ancestor, James Stafford.

# Robert Stafford

This is the story of Robert Stafford of Wayne and Glynn Counties born in 1765 and descended from William Stafford who emigrated from England to Virginia in 1622.

(Let us hasten to explain to students of coastal Georgia history who might have heard of another Robert Stafford [1790-1877] of Cumberland Island. Prominent banker, cotton planter and land baron, this shrewd businessman acquired much of his great wealth through foreclosure proceedings and sheriff's sales. There is substantial documentation of Stafford's humble origin and convoluted life.)

Robert Stafford, the subject of this essay, was Carolina born to Martha and Joshua Stafford who settled in St. Peter's Parish, Granville, South Carolina. Father and son both served in the American Revolution as members of the South Carolina militia for approximately six months each and their respective war claims were paid out in April, 1785.

Soon, the family migrated to Effingham County, Georgia where they became associated with the Earl and Blair families. In 1791, Robert Stafford married Jane Blair whose parents had served the Patriot cause and had been awarded 250 acres of land in Washington County for having furnished supplies to the Army and for military service.

Stafford seems thereafter to have worked as a surveyor helping in the definition of county boundaries. One map surviving from that period carries his signature of approval and certification of "the dividing line between Burke and Screven Counties." He also held office as a Justice of the Peace of Screven County from 1793-1799.

In 1810 Robert Stafford moved on to the County of Glynn and Wayne and a few years later traded 250 acres in Effingham for 300 acres in Glynn and Wayne. A decade later he was Justice of the Inferior Court in Wayne County with jurisdiction over such matters as estates, wills, marriage licenses, public roads and bridges, ad valorem taxes, business licenses--some of the affairs of a modern-day Board of Commissioners. He and his wife raised seven children who eventually married into the Wiggins, Hatcher, Ratcliff, Burney, O'Neal, McDonald, Walker and Bryant families.

On February 1, 1829 Robert Stafford signed his last will and testament. His 350 acre tract on the Post Road near the Buffalo Swamp went for lawful debts. His wife and sons received 450 acres in Irwin County. The inventory of his large estate lists a branding iron, three cotton gins, one linen wheel, two spinning wheels, one clock, a tea kettle, livestock.

The Staffords were a fixture on the Post Road, that famous passage along an ancient Indian trail by which wiregrass pioneers headed into the interior, travellers bound for Florida and stagecoach traffic. The historian Margaret Cate left this epitaph: "Stafford lived and died on the old Post Road--at Tuckerville, the first county seat of Wayne County, later known as Lott and now called Whitaker, a station on the A.B. and C. Railroad just above Thalmann." The surveyor, Robert Stafford, would doubtless have approved of that precision.

# Georgia "Cajuns" Rest at
# Camden's Oak Grove Cemetery

Just imagine, Cajuns in southeast Georgia! It is a sad but true tale that storytellers relate about the tragic plight of the banished Acadians. The 19th century American poet Henry Wadsworth Longfellow popularized the fate of exiled Acadians in his poem about the "gentle Evangeline." Few people know that a large population of French-speaking folk settled in early coastal Georgia. These refugees from Canada along with a smaller number from Santo Domingo, brought a cosmopolitan flare to the famed sea islands and south Georgia piney woods.

You might just wander through St. Mary's historic Oak Grove Cemetery (ca. 1788) and gaze upon the antiquity of the tombstones. Surnames near or within the walled "tomb of the Acadians" note the resting spot of some of Camden's earliest families. Bachlott, Dufour, Desclaux, Cormie, Vocelle, Carbon and Comeau. Inscribed in French, a headstone in memory of Margurite Comeau records that she was native to Acadia and died in her 80th year in February 1829.

Appropriately, in 1930 Camden's historian James Thomas Vocelle published a memorial book called *The Triumph of the Acadians: A True Story of Evangeline's People.* Mr. Vocelle recommended that those who read his book be inspired "to greater examples of loyalty and devotion to conviction and principle and imbue in each and every one of us a greater spirit of charity and tolerance toward all men, irrespective of race, color or creed."

Margurite Carbon Comeau was his paternal great-great grandmother. Vocelle's blood relation to the other chief families of Grand Pre, such as Thibadeau and LePrince only stimulated his interest and inquiry about his Nova Scotian ancestry.

Separated from her parents as a young child, Margurite never again saw them. Her wanderings took her to Santo Domingo where she fled from rebellion, and later to Charleston, South Carolina and the coastal seaport at St. Mary's, Georgia.

Where is Nova Scotia? And, what circumstances caused Margurite Comeau's displacement from her native Acadia?

Historically occupied by Micmac Indians, the Canadian maritime province of Nova Scotia connects by a narrow strait to the eastern

Canadian mainland of New Brunswick province. On its northwestern shore is the famed Bay of Fundy, where right whales swim and the greatest "ebb and flow of tides" worldwide occur. This important strategic area on the Atlantic seaboard guards the southern entrance to the Gulf of St. Lawrence.

In 1604 a small colony of French settlers arrived in this magnificent and fertile land. Initially, a nobleman of the French court of Henry IV sponsored this enterprise. Awarded a monopoly of the lucrative pelt and hide trade, Timothe Pierre du Guast, Sieur de Monts, immediately capitalized on his investment. Called the "Minas French" because of their concentration in the region of the Basin of Minas, these hardy folk exploited the fertile valley of Gaspereau. Many emigrated between 1632 and 1651 from the west of France, "a country of marshes."

In Acadia, they reclaimed New World marshes to raise grain and cattle; on the uplands, they cultivated orchards of pears, plums, cherries and apples. In addition to trade, game animals and the harvest of the sea supplemented their food quests.

In 1622, King James I of England awarded "Acadia" to a Scot, Sir William Alexander. He changed the name to "Nova Scotia" or "new Scotland." Soon, the beautiful land became a pawn in the Anglo-French struggle for empire. Finally, by the Treaty of Utrecht on April 11, 1713 the French formally ceded Acadia to the British. Subjugated "Acadians" requested permission to remain in their homeland. They wished to practice their Roman Catholic beliefs and to not bear arms against their French brethren. Because of their faith and their nationality, these French speakers suffered terrible persecution.

On July 28, 1755 Nova Scotian Gov. Charles Lawrence issued a deportation order for the Acadians. Approximately 4,000 people lived near Port Royal, present-day Annapolis Royal when this exile began. On October 27, 1755 Col. John Winslow implemented the order with the first forced transport from Minas.

Although the Acadians "scattered from one end of the Atlantic seaboard to the other," many sought refuge in Louisiana and came to be called "Cajuns."

But here is proof that this migration made its way to the Georgia coast: the Acadian ground in Oak Grove. Today, we may only speculate on the richness of Margurite Comeau's long and troubled life. She rests at the moss-draped Oak Grove Cemetery, near the golden ripening marshes of Camden in the old seaport village of St. Mary's, Georgia.

# The Shaking Quakers in Glynn &
# Camden Counties

In 1898, a small group of "shaking Quakers" from Union Village (Warren County), Ohio near Cleveland purchased a large tract of old rice lands in north Glynn County, formerly owned by the planter James Hamilton Couper. At the instigation of their sect leader, Dr. Joseph Slingerland, the Shakers acquired Hopeton-Altama plantation under conditions of depressed land prices.

A year later, they purchased a 716-acre tract from L. T. McKinnon at White Oak, located in northern Camden County. At their primary residence, approximately 30 members cultivated corn, pumpkins, sweet potatoes, melons and other garden vegetables for subsistence and sale. In October 1899 these hardworking, thrifty folk boasted a $10,000 rice harvest in Glynn County.

"Do all your work as though you had a thousand years to live and as you would if you knew you must die tomorrow." This guiding principle determined the soundness of their building construction, in churches, dwellings and farm buildings.

Their motto, "Hands to work and hearts to God," dictated the simplicity of design in their famous "Shaker furniture" and zeal for cleanliness and order.

Vigorous demonstration of ecstatic religious practices earned them the name of the "shaking Quakers." The members called themselves The United Society of Believers in the Second Appearance of Christ and were organized in England in the mid-1700s. Led by "Mother Ann" Lee, considered a female Messiah, a band of eight members immigrated to America in 1774 and settled near Albany, New York.

Thereafter, they successfully established small communities throughout New England and the northeast, and spread into the Midwest. However, certain religious tenets of this sect almost assured its doom. Segregation of the sexes in all aspects of everyday life and a code of celibacy discouraged acts of procreation. Subsequently, the Shakers relied upon converts to multiply and increase their numbers. Their compassion for orphans became legendary.

In Camden County, welcomed as good neighbors because of their friendliness, honesty and peaceable nature, the Shakers' plain clothing outwardly manifested their austere ways. They held property in common, and elders tutored and trained the children by separating the sexes. Although children attended public schools, home instruction prepared youth to assume occupations useful for the good of the colony.

The 1900 census records of Camden County in the 270th district of Tarboro shed some light on the membership of the Shaker colony. For instance, four middle-aged men were listed as heads of household: William Reynolds, Francis Carry, George Hutto and Joseph Comas, ages 58, 67, 51 and 55 respectively.

Female and male boarders were Clarra Hutto, age 17, Hardea Hutto, a male 14 years of age and Paul Hutto, 8 years, Allice Caldwell, age 16 years, and Maud Lawless, age 11 years shared room and board in this household of 11 persons with Napolean B. Brown, 62 years and Frank A. Smith, 11 years.

During a short residence in southeast Georgia the Shakers' overriding goal remained unmet. They failed to increase their number through converts, and so on October 4, 1902 the Shaker business manager Richard T. Clark sold their holdings in Camden County. Eventually, the late Clyde L. McCarthy, Sr. incorporated the former McKinnon-Shaker place into his substantial properties.

Today, the old White Oak Inn stands as a silent witness to the former presence of a nearby Shaker community. Its late innkeeper Mrs. George Varnadoe Baker chronicled her neighbor's residence and eventual departure in a manuscript deposited at the Georgia Historical Society in Savannah.

"They sold lots of beautiful antique furniture, and I have one of the marble top dining tables. For several days while the sale was going on, the roads were full of wagons with furniture coming from the Shaker place."

In Glynn County, the Shaker lands passed to notable families and businessmen, including the Duponts, Cator Woolford of Atlanta and the Jones family of Sea Island. Nonetheless, the Shaker presence in southeast Georgia enriched the tapestry of our coastal history.

# Coming
# Of Age

# On the Waterfront: Cook Bros. & Co. Sawmill and General Store

*Photo courtesy of Mrs. George H. Cook, Jr. & Fred Cook*

"And now comes the news that Brunswick goes back to sun time next Saturday night at 12 o'clock, so that Sunday's bells will again ring by means of sun time. The advocates of standard time applied to the wrong body to get what they wanted. If they had gotten Cook's mill whistle to consent to blow at 6:30 and 11:30 a.m. and 12:30 and 5:30 p.m., they would have the more easily fixed the matter. Cook's mill regulates the time of this town." –Brunswick Council, May 17, 1888.

A vital source of coastal history in Glynn County is the Cook family, Mrs. George H. Cook, Jr., who shared her memories of old Brunswick and son, Fred Cook, teacher, archeologist, and author of *History of the Sir Thomas Cook Family: Chapter 4, The Mill Years (1866-1896) (1992)*. With a natural ease born of growing up absorbing tales of local history, Mrs. Cook told me about the burl walnut Seth Thomas Regulator Clock, ca. 1850~1860 that hangs on her living room wall, and still keeps perfect time. It once regulated the time of the town.

"This clock was the official time piece for the city of Brunswick before the old City Hall (ca. 1890) clock. Cook Brothers blew their whistle by the clock and the townspeople set their time by it!"

Affordable waterfront property, cheap labor and a willingness to work, rail transport and an eye for opportunity brought the three Cook brothers from Worcester, Massachusetts to Brunswick, Georgia. In March 1866 John and Samuel Cook heeded a clarion call which beckoned them to coastal Georgia. Their response was to the cutting of yellow pine, a booming business in Georgia's piney woods interior.

John's occupation as bookkeeper for "John R. Cook and Brother Grocers" prepared him to assume responsibility for company coffers, and brother George disposed of the grocery business prior to his southward move. Samuel's role as overseer in the mill kept it "going at full speed." Even before the first board was sawed, a lack of collateral in the North, and the reluctance of bankers to become involved in a distant southern enterprise, nearly doomed the fledgling business. On March 31, 1866, a promissory note and mortgage deed on water lot #34 in Brunswick conveyed this property from Gustavus Friedlander for $1,000 to Cook Brothers and Company. In addition, a family loan and mortgage of the property to Sumner Cook empowered the brothers, and their partners William Moore and Warren A. Fuller to pursue business on the Brunswick waterfront.

Partner William Moore quickly vanished from the business, and by 1876 Warren Fuller moved to St. Simons Island and was associated with The Dodge Lumber Company, as popularized in his daughter's (Abbie Fuller Graham) scrapbook collection titled *Old Mill Days*, St. Simons Mills, Ga., 1874-1908 (1976), and in the novel *The Beloved Invader* by the late beloved novelist Eugenia Price.

Yellow pine was, initially, the chief raw material sawn by the company, and when Mr. J.J. Lissner retired from his chandlery business, Cook Brothers quickly filled this void. In 1884, the company solely outfitted the wooden, tall-masted sailing ships, which sailed into the port of Brunswick to engage in international commerce. By 1875, the local paper *The Brunswick Advertiser and Appeal*, T. G. Stacey, editor and proprietor, had begun publication. We gain insight into the variety of commodities, activities of "Cook Brothers & Co." and the family's involvement in community affairs from select news articles and advertisements. For instance, an 1879 ad exhorted the public to "Reduce Your Living Expenses! Buy all you can with your money! At Lowest Market Prices!"

Among other standard items, Cook Bros. & Co. offered cocoa nut candy, lemons, graham flour, ginghams and calicoes, boots and shoes, canned goods, apples and apple cider, Edam or Holland Cheese, dairy butter, buckwheat self-rising flour, hosiery, pocket cutlery, and razors.

"The Cook store sold a wide variety of items, providing literally everything required by the citizens of the Old Town for their daily lives." They issued commissary notes as "Cook Bros., & Co. General Commission Merchants and Manufacturers of Yellow Pine Lumber."

During the prosperous years of the 1870s, Cook Brothers Sawmill sawed and shipped 10,000,000+ feet of lumber annually. Fred Cook has described the first mill as "an attractive white building about 35 feet tall, 30 feet wide and 140 feet long. Its single sheet iron chimney was supported by cables attached to the roof and ground."

On May 16, 1877 a news brief noted that John R. Cook had been appointed Brazilian vice-consul in the port; later, he served for many years as city alderman. John and wife Mary's comfortable home in "Yankee-ville" was located at 716 Union Street (908 Union).

Brothers John and Samuel, charter members of the First Presbyterian Church on George Street, donated $1,000 and all of the lumber needed toward its construction. Through the early 1880s, their business expanded, but on December 13, 1884 a devastating fire destroyed the main building.

Again, family loans enabled the Cook brothers to rebuild and rise "phoenix-like" from ashes. By 1886, they had acquired one-half interest in the large McDonald sawmill, located near the rails of the Brunswick and Western (B & W) Railroad, 30 miles west of Waycross. But a combination of events conspired against the business, including increased competition and rail rates, and a subsequent decline in the profitability of sawmilling.

In 1888, the "Cook's Store" was sold to Andrew Mason and Company. Mason was the former sales manager for the store, but within a few years, his business failed. Samuel Cook died in 1890 and Brother John in 1896. A new sawmill and lumber business called "Kennon and Cook" operated at the foot of London Street, with Henry T. Kennon, a former cotton mill operator as a senior partner.

In 1898, the old mill operated under the ownership of Southern Pine Company, and by 1908, according to the Sanborn Fire Maps, the business had completely vanished. This was a far cry from the heyday of the late 1870s, when "Cook Brothers & Company" supported over seventy families, "fed and clothed through the business of this firm, either directly or indirectly," and when an old clock allowed the townspeople to set the time of the town.

# A Vanishing Historic Landscape and Brunswick's Old City Hall

*Photo courtesy of Steele Studios, Beaufort, S.C.*

Few century old buildings stand today in Brunswick's Downtown commercial district. A 1960s "progressive" urban renewal destroyed most of the original structures. But a lone sentinel exists on a vanishing historic landscape. Encompassed by the Old Town Brunswick Historic District, Brunswick's Old City Hall (ca. 1890) was listed on the national register on April 3, 1979.

National register boundaries correspond on the northward to H Street and include Magnolia Park, the old Courthouse (ca. 1907), and some residences of New Town; First Avenue on the south, Bay and New Bay Streets on the west, and Cochran Avenue (Martin Luther King, Jr. Boulevard) on the eastward.

While it continues to serve the needs of government, for instance, Recorder's Court, Old City Hall is a unique coastal Georgia landmark, in desperate need of restoration. In fact, it is the second oldest standing public building in Glynn County. Its history sheds considerable light on the regional circumstances of Brunswick-Glynn between 1880 and the turn-of-the-century Georgia.

The Richardsonian-Romanesque style features a masonry structure and a large, rounded arch at its entranceway. A conical roofline with encircling windows and rough cut granite stone work include other aspects of the style, not widely seen in the American South.

We can look into the "Proceedings" of Brunswick's City council for the auspicious circumstances under which Old City Hall was conceived. January 1889: "Brunswick is not the little town it once was, but a thriving, growing city, whose growth necessitates an increase of expenditures and causes a floating debt of some $10,000 which is represented by property of greater amount, saying nothing of the lands contributed, for the encouragement of manufacturing enterprises."

On January 6, 1890 city fathers entered into a contract to build a structure representing the "seat of government" and civic activities. Designed by a coastal architect whose buildings grace historic districts in North Carolina and in Georgia, Brunswick's Old City Hall was contracted at $33,000. Messrs. Anderson and Sharp were awarded the bid for construction.

In Savannah, Alfred S. Eichberg (1859-1921) the coastal architect, had designed a number of both commercial and residential structures, notably the Central of Georgia Railroad building, located at 233 West Broad Street, and the J.S. Wood home at 803 Whitaker Street in Savannah. In Wilmington, a newly restored New Hanover County

Courthouse (ca. 1892) boasts Eichberg's design. In Brunswick, other than Old City Hall, the campus of Glynn Academy features an Eichberg building: the Glynn Academy Annex, or Old Prep High (ca. 1905).

Along the Georgia coast, Eichberg's architectural work spanned tremendous growth--a 285% population increase in Glynn County between 1880-1890! Subsequent demands on municipal government, and especially those parties responsible for streets, drains and bridges, strained the budget.

On the other hand, tourism and trade promotion, railroad expansion and development enhanced both local and regional coffers. In December 1888 a curious feature article on the port city appeared in an edition of *Harper's Magazine Advertiser*. The writer promoted the healthful virtues of "Brunswick-by-the-Sea." "Brunswick gets a daily benefit of two of the best health-giving winds in the world. There is absolutely no better atmosphere anywhere than that of the pinewoods or that of the ocean. When the two are combined, as they are at Brunswick, there could be nothing more beneficial to persons in all conditions of health." Reflecting the purchase of Jekyll Island by a group of northern industrialists, the writer thought that Brunswick was destined to be the winter Newport of America.

In Brunswick-Glynn, the chartering of six banks in a ten year period, between 1884-1894 suggested great glory days, as an aftermath of dreary Reconstruction politics. Prospects were never better for a high standard of living, central to the fabric of life in our community.

Within this context, Old City Hall was built to reflect those aspirations of enduring stability and community achievement in a period of unprecedented growth and prosperity in "Brunswick-by-the-Sea."

In a world beset by often chaotic change, old buildings and reminiscences of the historic past connect us with our unique southern landscape. Even those planners, who designed "urban renewal" with all good intentions, left standing a lonely sentinel on the vanishing historic landscape. And in its essence, Brunswick's Old City Hall connects us with our rich heritage--the hallowed Southern past, and our most precious 'sense of place.'

# Heritage Stories and Africanisms
# On the Gullah Coast

*Photo from the "Ruby Berrie Collection"*
*Bryan-Lang Historical Library*

February is African-American History Month in the United States whereby stellar figures, such as Harriett Tubman, Booker T. Washington and the redoubtable George Washington Carver, have become household names to a popular (and young) audience who may not know of the achievements of this distinguished company.

Along the coast of Georgia, residents live with quite visible evidence of the 'first' Africans, and their impact on our everyday world. Even today and far removed from a plantation economy, the term "Africanisms" remains a viable one in the context of contributions to coastal lifestyles. You might think about this when next relishing the delicious culinary delight known as "gumbo" or when browsing antique markets for the expertly crafted "rice fanners" made of sweet grass and pine straw. You might talk with the old timers on the islands, who recall the small, free ranging horses which once frequented the barrier islands.

Among the Gullah-speaking, the term "tacky" applies and in this blend of English and African language, the word means "little horse." Enjoy the cadence of the local "Sea Island Singers" when they perform the old work and play songs. Each mid-August, the Sea Island Festival promoted by Frankie Sullivan Quimby and Doug Quimby celebrates music and song and other delights.

Learn the names of the "gone but not forgotten" who contributed so largely to a rich and shared heritage. Have you ever heard of a man named Old Quarterman? What about amateur folklorist and musicologist Lydia Parrish? The wife of famed illustrator Maxfield Parrish, "Miss Lydia" lived in a small cabin near the bloody marshes at Kelvin Grove.

Captivated by the richness of certain personalities, including "Miss Julia" and Joe Armstrong, Parrish determined to collect and record the old spirituals which, in the 1930s, were quickly disappearing from the coastal landscape. Professional anthropologists and musicologists recognize the shout and ring play songs as survivals of the African homeland.

Have you heard "Oh Eve--where is Adam?" What about the ring play song titled "Emma You My Darlin"? Filled with treasures, Parrish's book titled *Slave Songs of the Georgia Sea Islands* and originally printed in 1942 provides a snippet of historical information on "Old Quarterman."

Wallace's mother was taken from the Butler's plantation by overseer Roswell King, and Wallace was born in Liberty County. Although his Quarterman surname occurs in Glynn County, old timers often associate it with residents of McIntosh and Liberty Counties. For many years, this writer has searched for any scrap of historic information about Wallace Quarterman. Long years ago, on Sapelo Island, the late raconteur, Ronaster Johnson and "Miss Annie" Walker wistfully talked about him. I had missed a man who was known far and wide for excelling at an important dance, little known today, called "the buzzard lope."

In a column titled "Seashore Chatter" and printed on Friday, November 14, 1930 the writer Mrs. Julia G. Morrison commented on the presence of newspaper publishers Patterson of *The Baltimore Sun* and Clark Howell of *The Atlanta Constitution*. They had visited Parrish's cabin studio, and were entertained with "eats" consisting of tea, hoecake and jam.

Mrs. Isabel Gordon expertly prepared the hoecake. The "singers" included Joe, Julia and Pauline Armstrong, Willis Proctor, Clarence Small, Cornelia Murphy, Sam and Isabel Gordon, Ben Davis and Bessie Cuyler who sang the old timey songs. Morrison stated that "Old Quarterman brought down the house with his shouting." In the photograph, perceive the quiet dignity of a man who had witnessed, and participated in vast social change. According to oral history, Wallace Quarterman's house was once located behind the First African Baptist Church (ca. 1859) at Frederica. St. Simons Island businessman Jasper Barnes remembered that the shell roads were maintained by him.

In the Harrington community, islander Neptune Whing contributed that he believed Quarterman buried in the old Village Cemetery near Musgrove Plantation. "He lived to be in his 90s, and was an old, old man when I was a child."

# An Old Country Store

*Photo courtesy of Mrs. Hazel McCarthy White*

We remember the tales told by our parents and grandparents about the unique qualities and central role of a country store in the ordering of their lives. The folks who operated these generations-old businesses stood vigilant to protect the interests of their customers who made possible a good livelihood.

Largely due to the growth of mega-stores, those country merchants and their family-owned enterprises are quickly becoming an aspect of Americana, an object of nostalgia. Still, the roots of a country store stand deeply embedded in southern soil. And in my mind, the Tarboro Mercantile Store in northern Camden County holds an important place in memories of a rural Georgia.

The name Tarboro was borrowed from a North Carolina town east of Rocky Mount a century ago, transformed to Tarborough on the Providence Road about 12 miles north of the present community of Tarboro. This happened because of one Leonidus T. McKinnon who brought a group of turpentine workers from North Carolina to work in Southeast Georgia's piney woods.

These tarheels carried with them the name of their old home and along with that the reputation of skilled workers. Since the Colonial era, North Carolinians had exploited the coastal plain by boxing pines for their resin. This early crude procedure which often resulted in the weakening and then destruction of the tree from rot, windstorm and disease forced this component of the turpentine and naval stores business to seek more land in South Carolina and Georgia. Hence the migration.

At the junction of the Owens Ferry, Refuge and Burnt Fort Roads, near the present and second Tarboro, a settlement called Forkville sprang up in response to a certain prosperity. Drilled by the Stafford Brothers, an artesian well powered a large water wheel for the operation of a grist mill. Useful for grinding corn--the staff of southern life--the overflow of the water wheel also offered a delightful swimming pool as an added attraction for adults and children alike.

Recalls Shirley Joiner Thompson, Camden County historian: "I was born at Forkville while Daddy (Marion Clayborn "Stub" Joiner) was running the blacksmith-grist mill there. Tom Bruce ran the grocery store part of the business. The building is still there. The well has been capped but there is still a big pond where the water comes up. And by the way, lumber used in building the structures in Tarboro came from the old Woodbine jail!"

In time, the two settlements merged and became Tarboro, an important center of trade and mercantile business along with turpentine and naval stores production.

A decisive factor in this story is the arrival of John C. McCarthy who came to teach in a local school and stayed on as a businessman, residing with his family at Idlewild, a retired plantation near Bickley Chapel. Most importantly, his son, Clyde L. McCarthy, Sr. allied himself with L.T. McKinnon in the mercantile interest. In 1927, another son, Edgar Allan Poe McCarthy bought out the McKinnon-McCarthy firm and soon erected a new store that stands today as the Tarboro Mercantile. Offering a line of credit to wholesale and retail customers, McCarthy befriended his neighbors and made a good living at the same time.

Hazel McCarthy White started working in her father's store about 1948 and took over its operation after his death in 1960. "When Papa was there, it was about the only business out at Tarboro. He ordered feed, seed and fertilizer from Birmingham, Alabama, and it was brought into Camden County by the boxcar load. He warehoused these bulk items in White Oak where we moved in 1927 when I was five years old. Sometimes two boxcar loads of Jim Dandy animal feed and Jim Dandy grits arrived at the same time in White Oak. One of the most popular sale items was yard goods. We sold cotton at ten cents per yard. We also sold wooden caskets. I'd go with Papa everywhere he'd let me go--to buy mules on Bay Street in Jacksonville, for instance. Papa was Justice of the Peace and I sat on the front bench in a one-room courthouse!"

Not all that long ago, when Hazel McCarthy was young, the sight of fox, rattlesnake, bear, bobcat and alligator was pretty routine. Just as was the transport around the county by oxcart, mule, horse and wagon and then automobile.

Hazel McCarthy White sold the Tarboro Mercantile in 1985 because of changing times. The old landmarks are still standing, Mrs White testified, but the pilgrims have moved on. Not long ago, however, news of the re-opening of the Mercantile reached this writer. Hope the mourners benches are still intact! I must go soon to search there for delicious red-rind yellow hoop cheese!

# Jim Peterson

*Photo by the author*

    A man named Jim Peterson cut a hard row to hoe. Even today, few folks will question his legacy of business savvy and success. In the recent past, many a young fellow pensively set out on the challenging road he travelled and measured his worth by Peterson's accumulation of vast real estate holdings and great wealth.

    In the early 1930's, Vincent Harris, a Camden County native and vocational arts teacher at the Old Colored Memorial School in Brunswick encouraged a promising favored student, Jasper Barnes. "You keep on and you'll be the next Jim Peterson."

    Peterson's legacy has long held my fascination because of his ownership of a popular Island nightspot called The Blue Inn. Oldtimers tell me that Louie Armstrong--Yes! played there and "blew the stars out of the sky at night."

Jasper Barnes has assured me that an all-female revue called "The International Sweet Hearts of Rhythm" packed the place. In fact, Brunswick and the Golden Isles have traditionally enjoyed the benefit of the best musicians. Woe the loss of the legendary Genoa Martin and his skill at attracting name bands!

This portrait of Jim Peterson is based on conversations with Jasper Barnes, the late Evangeline P. Wallace, the educator Richard Perry, Oscar Thomas and Peterson's dearly beloved niece, Mrs. Ella Louise Atkinson. I've also looked into the City Directory of Brunswick and records from Judge Bernice Gilder's Glynn County Probate Court.

Jim Peterson was born on May 5, 1866 during the chaotic days of Reconstruction and the aftermath of the American Civil War. Reared in Albany, Georgia, he appears in public records in 1905 as a Glynn County businessman. At that time he and his wife, Elizabeth, lived at 514 Monk Street and operated a saloon at 112 Monk St. By 1908, Peterson operated a grocery store and meat market at 116 Monk. Over the next half-dozen years, Peterson lived on Wolf Street and maintained the grocery on Oglethorpe. In 1918, the Petersons were resident at 1528 Stonewall in Brunswick.

Richard Perry recalls that Peterson "raised and peddled vegetables on St. Simons Island and then got into the barroom business where he made money." Jasper Barnes believes that he sold watermelons and tomatoes from a harvested island farm.

In 1921 Peterson is listed in the City Directory as a real estate agent. His wife, Elizabeth, had died that year, mourned by her niece, Ella Atkinson: "My Aunt Lizzy was a smart wife and the woman behind Jim Peterson's success."

In the years following, Peterson resided on Lee Street and operated a substantial real estate business from a famous brick building in the 1400 Block of Gloucester St.

Richard Perry: "Jimmy Buggs was the contractor for the Peterson building. The Palace Theatre was located upstairs where there was also a dance hall. In later years there was a real estate office for Jim Peterson. Downstairs was cut into stores. Earl Hill operated The Green Lantern Grill. The Mock Brothers opened a grocery store and fruit stand well remembered by locals."

Late in life, Peterson married Carrie Wilson whom he met in Fernandina Beach. When Peterson died in 1941, "probably the largest Negro property owner in Brunswick," his widow filed suit for the administration of his estate. Peterson had died intestate and the subsequent litigation in the settlement of his large estate mostly consumed it. In particular his son, Hervy "Spurge" Peterson and widow Carrie came to no agreement and so carried their case far afield from Judge Edwin Dart's Glynn County Court of Ordinary.

Attorney W.C. Little was appointed permanent administrator and thereafter accounted for the collection of real estate rental income, purchase fees and the disbursal of necessary expenses incidental to upkeep. In May 1942, a rendering in the Glynn County Superior Court decreed that Hervey had "a full interest as a son and heir in the estate of J.S. Peterson."

But the heirs litigated and discord and bitterness ruled the day. The case finally was heard by the Georgia Supreme Court which, in December, 1943, ruled for Hervey. For the remaining twenty years of her life, Carrie Peterson lived with the controversy these trials engendered.

Jim Peterson rests today in Greenwood Cemetery under a concrete obelisk inscribed "Peterson 1915." His mother-in-law is there, as is his first wife, Elizabeth. Nearby, his widow, Carrie, lies in the Boles plot with her brother and her father, the Reverend William Boles.

One more legacy: the Peterson building still stands on Gloucester St. It now houses "Victorian Place," a popular antique shop in Brunswick today.

Success---Jim Peterson would be proud.

# Justine Lattany

*Photo courtesy of the Lattany Family &*
*Mrs. Phorestine Appling*

The late Viola D. Hummings of Woodbine inspired me to learn about the circumstances of rural midwives in Glynn and Camden Counties. Many of these women raised large families of their own in remote areas. The tradition or folk custom which dictated that the new mother stay in the birthroom for one month after the child was delivered meant that the midwife would remain with her for the duration.

Black midwives often served white and black communities though their pay, meager at best, varied. Mrs. Hummings records that "In the early years whenever they received money, the fee was $3.00." The midwives accepted "country pay," by and large, farm products, as a substitute for currency.

The knowledge and skills associated with midwifery were frequently passed from mother to daughter and granddaughter. So it was that the continuity of community was in tandem with the continuity of family tradition.

Among the statistics that Mrs. Hummings shared was this: that a woman named Justine Lattany of Red Cap Community delivered 97 live births in a twenty-five year period between 1910 and 1935.

"Justine of Red Cap?" Curious names always piqued my curiosity. Who was this woman and what were the conditions of her life?

Located about four miles west of Waverly in the sandhill section along the Post Road, Red Cap reflects the habit of coastal folk for succinct or very literal expressions. Fortunately, Mr. M.A. Knight of Brunswick clarified the origin of the name. After the Revolutionary War, horse racing became an important sport for the local boys. One day, a well-dressed stranger wearing a red British military cap and silver buckles on his pants and spurs, stopped to talk with the local folk. The stranger was challenged to a race. On the way, his horse shied and he was thrown and instantly killed when his head hit a big pine tree. He was buried in the woods bordering the narrow roadway with a wooden cross topped with his red cap placed as a marker.

I am indebted to relatives and friends of Justine Lattany for these details about her life: her surviving children, John Quincy and Evelyn Bernice of Red Cap; her granddaughter, the educator Phorestine Appling, the late Mrs. Hummings and Jasper N. Lang, formerly of Wayside Plantation.

Justine Lattany was born on April 11, 1877, squarely in the midst of Reconstruction politics in deep, rural Georgia. Across her long life, she witnessed great change in the social and economic conditions incidental to southern living--its southern fabric. She married William Lattany, a turpentine woodsrider twenty-six years older than she by whom she had twelve children.When Lattany died in 1924, four of their children were still dependent on their mother for support and sustenance.

John Quincy Lattany was two years old at that time. He explains how they were able to survive at Red Cap in the swamps and piney woods of southeast Georgia. "Everywhere you looked, there were big gardens and farms all over this place and they worked them! We harvested corn, pulled fodder and dug potatoes and helped our white neighbors, such as the Edgy family. We plowed in the fields. My first work was when I was 12 years old, dipping turpentine. Yeah, that's how we lived out there, doing a little farming and working turpentine and cutting cross-ties. We burned the woods before March15 when we started working turpentine again. We weeded boxes three feet around the tree so that the fire wouldn't burn it. For this [and the sixteen mile round trip walk to Waverly] we received twenty cents per 100 boxes weeded."

Evelyn Bernice Lattany became an expert fisherman; often her mother, Justine, allowed her to leave the fields early so that the child could hurry to the nearby fresh-water branch to catch the evening meal.

Mrs. Appling remembered her grandmother Lattany as a caring, understanding woman who actively served as a volunteer community worker and as a very responsible midwife. "There was no color barrier. She delivered children for both her black and white neighbors, including the Edgy, Wainwright, Rozier and Lang families." Her work took her across four Georgia counties and home to Red Cap. The families of that early twentieth century hamlet, the Lemons, the Smarts, the Jacksons, the Life and the Williamses, in their rural isolation depended on one another, strengthening their sense of community and place and a strong instinct for survival.

Not far from Red Cap, Justine Lattany rests today at Salter Cemetery where she was buried on June 16, 1964.

# Abundant Forest Resources:
# Turpentine Stills and Naval Stores

*Photo courtesy of Charles S. Tait, Sr.*

A large, impressive granite and bronze monument stands in the northwest quadrant on Queen's Square near old Brunswick City Hall. Tucked snugly under a very old spreading magnolia, a flurry of activity once centered on the economics and exchange at Brunswick Farmer's market located today at Mary Ross Harbor Market.

Friends and business associates--the Naval Stores Producers-- erected this marker in tribute to Columbia Downing and as an expression of their esteem and affection for his good works. Born in Dowington, Ohio on February 1, 1845, Downing later organized the lucrative Downing Company in Brunswick during the halcyon days of the early 1890's. He remained its president and actively participated in the business operation until his death on August 29, 1924.

Dateline--Brunswick, Ga. July 16, 1936, and the correspondence of The Downing Company, Inc./Naval Stores Factors and Wholesale Supplies sheds some light on the centering of an important naval stores business in Georgia. Facts pertinent to the operation of the business provide insight into the state of affairs, trade and economics along the Georgia coast.

Company vice-president C.P. Dusenbury responded to a query posed by Mrs. K.G. (Ruby) Berrie and the Brunswick Board of Trade. He noted "The Downing Co., Inc. will handle this year probably as many as 60,000 units of naval stores, that is 60,000 casks of spirits of turpentine, and 200,000 barrels of rosin, more than three-fourths of which will come to Brunswick."

Dusenbury commented that present prices were low, but that the company would sell $2.5-3 million dollars worth in 1936 for the benefit of their customers. "The proceeds of which are used by these producers of naval stores in operating their businesses, and the money passed back to the naval stores operators with which to pay their labor, operate their places and keep their business going."

On the Brunswick waterfront, in June 1936 The Downing Co. shipped approximately 24,000 barrels of rosin and 6,000 barrels of turpentine, by steamers bound for an international destination. Dusenbury opined that "the naval stores business seems to be gradually centering in Georgia."

Not long ago, I talked about the Tarboro Mercantile Co. with Mrs. Lloyd (Hazel McCarthy) White of Camden County, daughter of its founder, E.A.P. McCarthy, who expressed a similar opinion. "Turpentine came into its own during the great Depression, then afterwards, timber became important in southeast Georgia, and later the products of coastal pulp mills."

Lumbering was one of the first important businesses in early Georgia, dating from Georgia's Trustee period (1732-1753). The exploitation of abundant forest resources included felling virgin stands of long-leaved pine, cypress, white oak, red oak and the maritime live oak forest. Industrious colonials shipped lumber, barrel staves and shingles to a European and Caribbean market. Numerous references in Georgia's *Colonial Records* document the liberal attitude of the Trustees in land granting, especially if the colonialist intended to erect a sawmill, or produced potash. Later, the port of Darien in McIntosh County prospered due to timber rafting from interior forests and Camden County river settlements grew along the Satilla River. Some of those settlements included Satilla Bluff, Ceylon, Bailey's Mill and Owen's Ferry, almost forgotten on the historic landscape today.

Sawmilling proved the backbone of these bustling communities and in response to the needs of the Dodge-Meigs Company, later the Hilton and Dodge Lumber Company of St. Simons Island. According to the late coastal historian Margaret Davis Cate, the Hilton and Dodge Lumber Co. "was the largest timber company active in the southeastern part of Georgia from 1874-1903."

By the 1920s, turpentining and the production of naval stores provided employment for a large segment of the coastal population. Whole families relocated from the Carolinas to coastal Georgia, and enormous fortunes were accumulated by shrewd businessmen. The importance of this lucrative business simply must not be overlooked by anyone remotely interested in the coastal economy.

The term "naval stores" dates to the colonial period when pine gum was cooked down to a thick tar, and the tar applied to preserve hemp rope, and to caulk the seams of ships. Spirits of turpentine results from a complicated distillation process, after the oozing gum has been collected from a "chipped" pine tree.

New Englanders exploited pitch pine for gum naval stores. By 1700, North Carolinians had discovered that the abundant long-leaf yellow pine was a more prolific producer of resinous gum. A wasteful practice of "boxing" pines for their oozing resin involved slicing a deep hole into the base of the tree where the crude gum resin gathered.

But a native of Milledgeville (Baldwin County), and chemist by trade, observed the inefficiency and wastefulness of this land-consuming practice. Charles Holmes Herty determined to rectify and revitalize the naval stores industry. Ultimately, in 1903, he patented a cup and gutter process that required a superficial "chip" and reduced the stress on the pine tree. A clay pot designed with a round bottom--the Herty cup--used in conjunction with galvanized iron gutters proved a useful adaptation for turpentine and naval stores producers.

Later, Herty played an instrumental role in the growth of the pulpwood industry in the American South. He encouraged businessmen to manufacture newsprint from young southern pines, and advocated the cultivation of slash pine for this purpose. His progressive approach to problem solving revolutionized the naval stores industry, and stimulated the southern economy.

In an April 1935 *Savannah Morning News* article Herty suggested "the possibilities of the pine industry in Georgia and of the great cattle industry that will come when we stamp out wiregrass with carpet grass." Progressive as he was, Herty was dated by the state of science and the period in which he lived.

Today through the efforts of the non-profit research station at "Tall Timbers" in Leon County, Florida, plant ecologists document the important ecological role of wiregrass. In the piney woods community where a dense growth of *Aristida stricta* (wiregrass) occurs, legumes will be found in great quantity. They provide an essential source of food for woodland creatures, which suggests the niche of this wiry, lowly plant in a naturally functioning system. It's a reminder of its usefulness as a food source for the free ranging cattle of early turpentine workers.

# Columbia Downing of
# The Downing Company

*Photo courtesy of Steele Studios, Beaufort, S.C.*

I have been long intrigued by all aspects of the workings of naval stores producers and factors, so my inquiry into the circumstances of Columbia Downing represented an essential pursuit especially when I considered his exercise of American energy, ability, integrity and superior skills evidenced by The Downing Company.

Although few people today are aware of Downing's mark on the landscape, his contributions to the citizens of southeast Georgia were enormous and far-reaching. In addition, as a naval stores factor and commission merchant, The Downing Company achieved new dimensions in economic prosperity and the subsequent growth of Brunswick's port traffic.

A Brunswick Board of Trade publication written and published by William S. Irvine in 1902 rightly boasted of the incomparable natural advantages of Brunswick...the second largest shipping port in the world for naval stores. Brunswick was, moreover, the leading shipping port for cross-ties and Columbia Downing was at the helm.

Born on February 1, 1845 into a prominent Meigs County, Ohio, family, Downing grew up on a farm near Middleport. His ancestors were early settlers thereabouts and from them, no doubt, he inherited their sense of responsibility to the community and a kindly benevolence. Downing attended college in Athens, Ohio, and then at Lombard University near Galesburg, Illinois, where he showed great promise in his business studies.

Here are two myths about Downing that we will encounter: one is that while he bore the title Major throughout his life, in fact it was a courtesy. He had served with the Union in the Civil War. Georgia's historian, Lucian Lamar Knight, recorded that he had been an artillery officer, brigade quartermaster and aide-de-camp, that he had been discharged as a First Lieutenant. Moreover, and perhaps most important, Downing did not come to Brunswick with the occupying forces!

Downing returned to Ohio after The War, a decade later married Mary Helen Remington who bore two daughters. By 1881, his work with Chess Carley Company, a predecessor of Standard Oil brought him to the South where he served as company representative in Atlanta and Savannah and soon engaged in the naval stores business. Shortly, Chess Carley quit the region whereupon Downing quit Chess Carley and organized a naval stores factorage house which, by 1884, had become C. Downing Jr. and Company. Thereafter in 1890, it was incorporated as The Downing Company. Other principals were R.W. Patterson, E.A. Buck, W.E. Burbage and J.J. Connoly. The charter resembled that of a bank because of the special banking in which the factorage engaged.

It is worth noting the similarity of ante-bellum Savannah rice factors and the business of a naval stores factorage such as The Downing Company. Both advanced money, the one to the rice planter, the other to the turpentine operators. Both conducted business with far-reaching implications.

Downing offered the naval stores operator or producer financial backing to bring naval stores crops such as resin and turpentine to market. Credit enabled the operator to purchase timber, necessary equipment and supplies, groceries and any other essentials. By the mid-1890s Brunswick had displaced both Charleston, South Carolina and Wilmington, North Carolina as a naval stores port and market. This development resulted from the shrewd business acumen of Columbia Downing who was simultaneously the President of the First National Bank organized in 1884, President of the fledgling Board of Trade and Director of the Oglethorpe Hotel Company.

Downing's philanthropy did not go unnoticed: *The Atlanta Constitution* on January 3, 1901 described just how The Downing Company's drays were kept busy for hours preceding Christmas Day hauling huge loads of hams, bacon, flour, crackers, delicacies, etc. to the local headquarters of the "Kings Daughters" for distribution to the Brunswick poor. His will made generous grants to the St.Marks Episcopal Church of Brunswick; the Brunswick Hospital; the Young Mens Christian Association and the Public Library Association of Brunswick.

Downing died in 1924 in Richmond Hill, New York, "unspoiled by wealth" as one Ohio newspaper offered. Two years later, the Downing Memorial Association, comprised of business associates, unveiled a monument in Queen's Square dedicated to their old friend "the late beloved and honored citizen, C. Downing."

In our time, the Downing home on Egmont, a Queen Anne structure, is owned by the Tzucanow family who operate a bed and breakfast there. After a fifty-six year long career, The Downing Company was liquidated on February 1, 1946. Its office building gave way in 1974 to a HUD urban renewal project. Miss Mary McGarvey, writing in Georgia's *Coastal Illustrated*, lamented the loss of that edifice which bore "a Dickensian setting where Dombey and Son might have done business. The tide advanced and retreated under the pilings and there were fireplaces in the offices and there was the great dim warehouse with all the rich smells."

Columbia Downing and his company encompassed a signal period of great confidence in our nation's potential for growth and production. Perhaps his parents anticipated his life with that name, "Columbia."

# Alfred Vincent Wood, Sr. —
# A Beloved Brunswickian

*Photo courtesy of Miss Clara Marie Gould*

No wonder that his descendants, kinfolk and followers place such a high premium on education. Alfred Vincent Wood, Sr. served as president of the Glynn County Board of Education for over twenty-five years! And surely his extended family's evening conversations revolved around the benefits of a life-long process of educating oneself. What sage advice!

Alfred Vincent Wood was born on October 3, 1853, in Wilmington, North Carolina to Mary Anne Wilbur and Robert Barclay Wood, formerly of Nantucket, Mass. Their great-grand-daughter, Mrs. King (Beverly Wood) Hart recalled that the decline in the New England whaling industry possibly accounted for the Wood family's move to the Carolina tidewater.

In 1877, Alfred V. Wood moved to Brunswick, and within four years, on December 14, 1881 married Marion Colesberry of Philadelphia, Pennsylvania. They were the parents of seven children, many of whose descendants are living today. In their lifetime, their father's business success enabled him to build an impressive, multi-storied frame home with Queen Anne affinities. When Gloucester Street featured residences of prominent Brunswickians, the Wood home including spacious grounds, tennis courts, a horse and buggy drive, and ornamental fountain, sprawled over the 1700 block of Gloucester. Ponder this when next visiting the Office Park complex, Revco Drug Co., and First Georgia Bank headquarters!

In a *Weekly Naval Stores Review* article (May 1, 1921) titled "Naval Stores--History, Production, Distribution and Consumption" the editor Thomas Gamble provided a glimpse of the career moves of Alfred V. Wood, Sr. He noted that John D. Sprunt of Wilmington pioneered as Brunswick's naval stores factor and conducted a small business in the port. Within three years, in 1879, A.V. Wood, Sr. succeeded Sprunt and within four years Major Columbia Downing arrived Downtown.

In Wood's fifty-six year career with the naval stores industries, he worked tirelessly for the promotion of those products and in service to the port and the Glynn County community. In fact, he served as manager of The Downing Company's yard between 1890 and April 12, 1926 when Wood died.

Today, locals recall yesteryear's bustling activities at the rosin docks, located at the foot of Gloucester Street. A thriving naval stores industry and the production of rosin and spirits of turpentine had supplanted cotton and rice as export commodities. A.V. Wood's strategic position in the midst of such a lucrative business empowered him to contribute, in humanitarian ways to the Glynn County community.

Among others, he served on the Brunswick Board of Health, the Glynn County Forestry Association, and was a trustee of the Georgia State Woman's College at Valdosta. Because of his interests in sanitation, he was appointed an honorary member of the Royal Medical College of England. Wood is best recalled for his interest in the provision of a quality education for local school children.

His granddaughter Miss Clara Marie Gould remembers hearing about the stimulating public lecture series or Chautauqua in turn-of-the-century Brunswick-Glynn. "My grandfather always purchased season tickets for the teachers at the four schools. These educators congregated near Brunswick's Old City Hall to benefit from the traveling Chautauqua."

In the archives of coastal historian Margaret Davis Cate, we catch a glimpse of Wood's participation in commencement exercises. A program of the Glynn Academy Graduation exercises held on June 8, 1920 at 8:30p.m. began with a chorus of "God of the Nations" by Verdi. Following an invocation by Rev. O.P. Gilbert, prominent Brunswickians James T. Colson, Louis H. Haym and Millard Reese gave short talks on vital school concerns. The graduating class of 1920 advocated a motto of "The past forever gone, the future still our own."

Class officers included President of the senior class, Palmer Smith, Vice-president Flora Isaac, Secretary Melvin Brockinton and Treasurer Ida Davis. Over these proceedings of pomp and circumstance and a class roll of nineteen students presided A.V. Wood, who, as president of the Board of Education awarded diplomas.

After his death, eulogies abounded which extolled Wood's civic contributions. "He was a friend to man, in his right hand carrying gentle peace...he has filled a pure life with the blessings of good deeds." Representing the Brunswick Woman's Club, Mrs. C.H. Leavy introduced a resolution to be published in the minutes of that service organization.

She remarked about the irreparable loss of a "highly esteemed Brunswickian, generous, high-minded, and a public spirited leader." In a feature news article about "A Leader Gone with A.V. Wood's passing," the writer captured the essence of a dedicated public servant. "As a public servant, he was without flaw, earnest, devoted, conscientious; serving without expectation of fee or reward except that rich remuneration of the man who has the constant realization of public duty well performed."

No higher compliment was accorded Wood's civic-minded nature than that of the famed coastal educator, Miss A. Jane Macon. In tribute to Wood's untimely death, Miss Macon told Glynn students about the life of this beloved man; if their paths followed his, success was assured in life. Wood's dynamic and diverse interests and civic-mindedness served as a role model. In fact, Wood's involvement in shaping the education of local youth assumed a regular pattern.He often visited in classrooms to interact with the youth whose lives he helped shape.

And he lectured on specialized learning with which he had familiarized himself. "He raised children to appreciate the wonder of the natural world," stated Miss Clara Marie Gould. What a tremendous gift to students who live in the biological wonder world of maritime live oak forests and teeming, spreading salt sea marshes!

# The Gifted Charles S. Tait, Sr.

*Photo courtesy Mrs. Margaret Tait Ratcliffe &*
*Mr. C.S. Tait, Sr.*

This is the story of Charles S. Tait, Sr. who moved to Brunswick with his bride Margaret from Gastonia, North Carolina in the 1880's where, in a region which delighted in its natural beauty, he became its most distinguished horticulturist. In time, the Taits raised eight children in their home on Dartmouth Street.

For over forty years, Tait worked for The Downing Company as manager of wholesale groceries but his great avocation was served in the family greenhouse. It is to his daughter, Mrs. Margaret Tait Ratcliffe who has since died, that I turn for the following details. One of Brunswick's most esteemed senior citizens, she was herself an acknowledged authority on cultivated evergreen shrubs and ornamental household plants.

"My father told me that from the time he was seven years old, he was interested in growing plants, especially flowering plants." As an adult, Tait rose early to work in the greenhouse which was heated by a coal-burning furnace. Nearby farmyard critters, cows and chickens, lazed in a Southend yard located between First Avenue and Dartmouth Street. The neighborhood was connected by streetcar with Downtown. From a backyard business grew Tait's Floral Company which was in time housed at 803 First Avenue across the street from the old Brunswick Hospital, a lucrative customer in the early years.

The Tait letterhead stationery noted that C.S. Tait, Sr. sold potted plants, bedding plants, cut flowers for all occasions, amaryllis and azaleas. Acclaimed as a "second Luther Burbank," Tait became famous for plant hybridization. The late attorney A.W. Fendig, Sr., who cultivated over 700 varieties of cameillas at his Orange Grove home on St. Simons Island, credited Tait with introducing him to the world of the *Cameilla japonica*!

For that matter, Tait is recognized as having launched the "Cameilla Fancy" in Glynn County, varieties of which bore such names as "Margaret Tait Ratcliffe," a semi-double, "Mrs. A.N. Shelander," a white semi-double; "Pearl King Tait"; "C.S.Tait, Sr." and a delicate pink variety known as "Tait's Masterpiece." "Tait's Ruffled Rose Azalea" went on the market as "Pride of Brunswick."

Tait and his partner and brother-in-law, R.H. Parker, eventually bought land at New Hope Plantation in the north section of the County where they grew bulbs. Margaret Tait Ratcliffe recalled vast fields where ten thousand amaryllis, narcissus and daffodil bulbs waited to be shipped round the world!

In 1894 C.S. Tait, Sr. published a guide entitled *The Seaside Gardener*. From his hobby of photography comes another legacy, hundreds of glass lantern negatives of the old days, many of them quite useful in reconstructing a historic landscape. Surely, the name Tait still rings true for those who seek quality garden products.

# Are Bells Ringing for Brunswick/Glynn County?

*Photo by the author*

A landmark tabby Spanish Mediterranean-Revival building (circa 1931) stands at the entrance to the Fernando J. Torras Causeway that leads to St. Simons/Sea Island. Located on the porch near the sign that proclaims "information" center is a large metal bell. It once played important roles in the daily affairs of the city, and therefore, the citizens of Brunswick-Glynn.

Impressed in the bronze bell is the name of the maker, John Benson from New York, 1850. My guess is that few of us are aware of this old bell, and its significance--an artifact of the ante-bellum past. And one of the more reliable accounts about its usefulness in yesteryear's daily affairs derives from a short essay called "The Bells/The Story of the Bells," written by Miss Maria C. Blain.

Miss Blain's father, James T. Blain, served as mayor of the city from 1859-1861, and his prominence in politics must have enhanced Miss Blain's awareness of history-making events. Prior to her death in January 1936 she recorded certain reminiscences about the dire circumstances of the Brunswick Riflemen and Brunswick-Glynn during the turbulent days of the American Civil War.

In her story about the bells, Miss Blain noted, "In 1857 Brunswick was a very different looking place contrasted with the Brunswick of 1929. Houses were few and far between." A tidal ditch ran along present-day Mansfield Street from Oglethorpe Bay to Reynolds Street. Straddling this deep ditch opposite the present old City Hall (circa 1890) was a marketplace, "a wooden structure, dignified by the name Market." In the belfry of the marketplace hung the bronze bell. Bell ringers announced the arrival of important cargoes of meat and vegetables in the port city. "Fresh meat was a rarity in those days. . .it was pathetic to see the people hurrying to secure a share. Sometimes there would be but a quarter of beef, never a whole one."

At the urging of General P.G.T. Beauregard, desperate for metal to manufacture Confederate artillery, Brunswickians rallied and sent four bells, including the market bell, to Macon, Georgia. For no known reason, the Brunswick bells remained unused, and in 1886, James T. Blain arranged for their return to the city by the sea.

Upon its arrival, the old market bell assumed a new duty when it hung over the fire department headquarters. Later, the old market place bell was transferred to a wooden scaffold located at the entrance to the city/Palmetto Cemetery whose sexton announced the evening closing of the cemetery gates with its toll.

Rescued from an ignoble fate when it lay in cemetery sands after the wooden scaffold deteriorated, the old market bell was removed to the newly completed "visitor's club," at the entrance to the causeway. A feature article in the local paper by city editor Deborah Clark noted that a winter visitor, Mrs. I.C. Hauscom of New Hampshire, took an interest in the history of the old market place bell and "through this interest" its prominent placement was assured. Its long legacy of community service continued as recently as July 4, 1966 when Mrs. Lillian Ames, president of the Altrusa Club, rang the old market bell at the causeway Chamber of Commerce building, having joined in a campaign to "make freedom really ring."

A nation-wide program encouraged each church, fire station and any organization with bells to ring them for two minutes beginning at 1 p.m. on Monday, July 4, 1966. This special event commemorated July 4, 1776 when the ringing of the Liberty Bell at Independence Hall announced the signing of the Declaration of Independence.

# Further Reading

Oldtimers enjoy any opportunity to reminisce about earlier days along the Georgia coast and the magic of coastal history. An awesome cast of characters who lived, loved, worked and died here will surely pique the interest of the banker and the beachcomber!

Certain stellar personalities such as Tallu Fish, Mary Ross, Margaret Davis Cate and Bessie Lewis eagerly promoted the mystique of the past, to determine for us the mysterious nature of those tabby ruins shrouded by old, old live oaks heavy-laden with eery Spanish moss. If you didn't know these ladies, here are a few books which possess a lure that beckons the curious, the romantic, the amateur historian.

My introduction to the history of coastal Georgia began with a lovely book by Caroline Couper Lovell titled *The Golden Isles of Georgia* published in 1933. Miss Lovell was the niece of Captain Charles Spalding Wylly, C.S.A. a native of McIntosh County and a descendant of numerous coastal luminaries including Thomas Spalding of Sapelo Island. Before his death in 1923, Captain Wylly had published a number of books about his family's place in the region, for instance, *Annals and Memoirs*. Moreover, the old veteran joined with the Brunswick DAR to erect the handsome Celtic cross which dominates the northeast quadrant of Queen's Square near Brunswick's old City Hall and which grounds our sense of place. The plaque at the base bears a dedication to James Edward Oglethorpe: "Lover of his fellow men, most ardently those of poor estate."

Two other seminal works in my education have been Margaret Davis Cate's 1930 treasure trove, *Our Todays and Yesterdays: A Story of Brunswick and the Coastal Islands* which foreshadowed Mrs. Cate's greatest endeavor, *Early Days of Coastal Georgia* (1955). This last volume captures the imagination, the essence, of a vanishing landscape and inspires the reader to a greater appreciation of the rich diversity of coastal history and heritage.

I must not forget Burnette Vanstory's *Georgia's Land of the Golden Isles* first released in 1956 and still in print from the University of Georgia Press.

A major scholar in coastal studies in recent years has been Virginia Steele Wood who is on the staff of the Library of Congress. Mrs. Wood has recovered and seen into publication three early narratives about our region. One is William Hazzard's *1825 St. Simons Island Georgia; Brunswick and Vicinity: Description and History*; Robert Durfee's *Journal and Recollections*, an 18th century record; and Jonathan Bryant's *1753 Journal of a Visit to the Georgia Islands of St. Catherine's, Green, Ossabaw, Sapelo, St Simons, Jekyll and Cumberland*, published with great style by the Mercer University Press and the Georgia Historical Society.

And there is a history of Brunswick, written and published by Colonel C.P. Goodyear in 1878. No copy seems to have survived but if you find one, do share!

Meanwhile, for the student-reader, here is a selected list of books used in the preparation of *Falling For Coastal Magic*.

Aronson, Peggy et al ed. *Camden's Challenge: A History of Camden County, Georgia*. Alpharetta, Georgia: 1994.

Betts, Edwin Morris. *Thomas Jefferson's Farm Book*. Charlottesville, Virginia: 1976.

------------------------ *Thomas Jefferson's Garden Book*: 1766-1824. Philadelphia: 1944.

Cate, Margaret Davis. *Our Todays and Yesterdays: A Story of Brunswick and the Coastal Islands*. Brunswick: 1926, 1930.

------------------------ Wightman, Orrin Sage. *Early Days of Coastal Georgia*. New York: 1955.

Connor, Jeannette T. ed. *The Whole and True Discouerye of Terra Florida* by Jean Ribaut. Gainesville, Florida: 1964.

Coulter, E. Merton ed. *Georgia's Disputed Ruins*. Chapel Hill, North Carolina: 1937.

Ellingson, Paul and Mendelson, Johanna. *Mary Letitia Ross Papers: A Descriptive Inventory*. Atlanta: 1979.

Eubanks, Thomas and Morgan, John. *Intensive Archaeological Testing at the John Houstoun McIntosh Sugarhouse, Camden County, Georgia.*

Atlanta: 1985.

Fish, Tallu. *Once Upon An Island: The Story of Fabulous Jekyll.* 1995.

Graham, Abbie Fuller ed. *Old Mill Days, 1874-1908.* Brunswick, Georgia: 1997.

Groover, Robert Long. *Sweet Land of Liberty: A History of Liberty County, Georgia.* Roswell, Georgia: 1987.

Hudson, Charles. *The Southeastern Indians.* Knoxville, Tennessee:1976.

Huxford, Judge Folks *Pioneers of Wiregrass, Georgia Vols I-IX.* Homerville, Georgia.

Johnson, Thomas. *The Herbal, or General History of Plants* by John Gerard. New York:1975.

Leslie, Mary Linda. *Margaret Davis Cate Collection: A Descriptive Inventory.* Atlanta: 1976.

Lovell, Caroline Couper. *The Golden Isles of Georgia.* Boston: 1932.

Parrish, Lydia. *Slave Songs of the Georgia Sea Islands.* Hatboro, Pennsylvania: 1965.

Vanstory, Burnette. *Georgia's Land of the Golden Isles.* Athens, Georgia: 1956.

Wood, Virginia Steele ed. *St.Simons Island, Georgia; Brunswick and Vicinity: Description and History by William W. Hazzard.* Belmont, Massachusetts: 1974.

----------------------ed. *Robert Durfee's Journal and Recollections.* Marion, Massachusetts: 1990.